MARTIN LUTHER

His Life and Teachings

JAMES ARNE NESTINGEN

FORTRESS PRESS   PHILADELPHIA

With thanks for my grandparents
Ingar and Malla Nestingen
Arne and Helma Vinge

The texts of Luther's Small Catechism and quotations of other Lutheran confessional documents are from *The Book of Concord*, translated and edited by Theodore G. Tappert (Philadelphia: Fortress Press, 1959).

Biblical quotations are from the Revised Standard Version of the Bible, copyright 1946, 1952, © 1971, 1973 by the Division of Christian Education of the National Council of the Churches of Christ in the U.S.A., and are used by permission.

Library of Congress Cataloging in Publication Data

Nestingen, James Arne.
  Martin Luther, his life and teachings.

    1. Luther, Martin, 1483–1546.
  2. Reformation—Biography. I. Title.
BR325.N47 1982   284.1′092′4 [B] 82–71829
ISBN 0-8006-1642-1

9589C82   Printed in the United States of America   1–1642

CONTENTS

FOREWORD

Who is Luther?

There are good reasons for asking such a question. But there is dispute—even among believers—about whether there is equal value in an answer.

November 10, 1983, marks Martin Luther's 500th birthday. For half a millennium he has remained a fascinating character, drawing the interest of the secular and the saintly, the contentedly irreligious and the faithful. His social, economic, political, and cultural significance has been repeatedly assessed. His personal development, psychological states, and understanding of the world have been scrutinized and debated. And his theological work remains the subject of constant analysis. In fact, it is commonly said that more has been written about Luther during these five hundred years than anyone except Jesus and the apostle Paul.

This sixteenth-century German monk, who taught in an obscure, frontier university and from this position got caught up in a swirling church reform, still has an explosive quality about him—even if he now lives only between the covers of a book. He is down-to-earth, warm and engaging, and as full of life as a busload of kids.

At the same time, Luther can be petty, outrageously maddening in his reflections on the faith, and intolerant in his treatment of others.

If nothing else, this fascination, this way of drawing interest—of both charming and enraging over all those years—

may provide a first reason for asking about Luther. What was he like that five centuries later he is still kicking over the traces?

Then there is the matter of Luther's legacy. A whole body of Christendom—the largest Protestant denomination in the world—has received its name from Luther.

Opinions about this legacy are mixed. Luther's legacy, after all, is not unambiguously Lutheran, at least not in the sense of carrying a direct and unbroken line from Luther himself. Many other people and many other forces, both at the time of the Reformation and since, have had a hand in shaping the Lutheran church. It is a basic error, even if a tempting one, to assume that the childrens' children—even to the fifteenth generation or the fifth century after—bear the exact likeness of one of the fathers.

Still, Luther continues to be named by and to name this large segment of the Christian church. His influence, however, is not confined to Lutherans. Some of the most significant twentieth-century studies of Luther, for example, have been done by Methodists and Roman Catholics.

So there is further reason to ask: Who is Luther? What was he up to that he has had such a shaping influence in the church? With such reasons for asking, are there equally good reasons for answering? After all, not everything that is of interest or even influential about Luther is worth pursuing. Strong arguments have even been presented in favor of forgetting Luther and therefore leaving this question alone.

Part of the reasoning behind the suggestion to forget Luther is left over from wartime propaganda. Luther is to the people of Germany what Thomas Jefferson is to the people of America, and what a combination of Sir John A. MacDonald and Louis Riel could be to Canadians. He is a founding influence, shaping not only attitudes but also the language itself.

With two world wars for evidence, particularly the English but also some Americans have argued that Luther must somehow be implicated. It is commonly said, for example, that

Luther absolutized the state and thus shielded it from the kind of criticism it should have gotten when the Nazis took power. Consequently, Luther is viewed as an authoritarian kind of thinker, out of place in a contemporary democratic context.

Another set of reasons for leaving Luther to obscurity is ecumenical. He was initially loyal to the papacy and even after conflict sought reconciliation with it. However, when Luther lost hope for the popes, he did not mince any words. He came to regard the papacy as the "Antichrist," the figure spoken of by Paul in the Thessalonian letters as Christ's principal opponent at the end of all things. From around 1520 until his death in 1546, with special venom in his later years, Luther unceasingly attacked the popes.

In an age of reconciliation, when Lutherans and Roman Catholics have achieved new levels of ecumenical understanding, the older Luther is often regarded as an embarrassment. The time has come, it is said, to move him out of the way of church progress.

At least an equally if not more painful point for Lutherans concerns Luther and the Jews. Particularly at the time when he was almost constantly ill and living daily with death, Luther wrote certain indefensibly vile tracts against the Jews. One of these, *On the Jews and Their Lies,* is regularly used by anti-Semites to prove their point and by their opponents to demonstrate Luther's bigotry.

A third set of reasons for not investigating the question of Luther is socioeconomic. One of the widely held assumptions of the academic world, the Weber thesis, lumps Luther together with John Calvin, another great sixteenth-century reformer. The common faith of Luther and Calvin is then considered a factor in the shaping of modern acquisitive capitalism. Consequently, Luther is viewed as part of the company that must accept blame for the ills of contemporary life: the uncontrolled growth of technology, pollution, covetousness as a way of life, and the like.

In addition, Luther is one of those held responsible for the excessive individualism of the Western world. By meeting his own need religiously, he started to unravel the string that holds individuals together in community.

There is a fourth problem that Luther poses—this one more particularly for the church. One of the watchwords of Luther's reform was "the word alone." This belongs with two other exclusive sayings of the reformer, "grace alone" and "faith alone." Together these three "alones" set out to declare the sole sufficiency of Christ, through the Word proclaimed in Scripture, to engender the faith of the new creation. The Scripture is its own interpreter, Luther insisted. No other souce or authority is needed to guarantee its interpretation.

If this is the case, why do Lutherans continue to fool with Luther? Having kicked the pope out of bed with the Bible, has Luther now crawled into the same bed, insisting that the Bible is his own book and that it has to be read his way? Do not Lutherans open themselves to the same charges that Luther himself leveled—that is, placing Luther or selected Lutheran writings between themselves and Scripture, or even more basically, between themselves and Jesus?

If there are reasons to ask "Who is Luther?" there are at least four, if not more, sets of reasons for putting this question aside. Some of the reasons for dismissing Luther however, are historically false. None of the four sets of reasons, not even Luther's attitude toward the Jews, is beyond discussion and dispute. Still, the reasons are all serious and of such a nature that if Luther cannot be dismissed, neither can the criticisms that have been leveled against him.

Maybe it is just the mixed nature of his reviews—adoring allegiance counterbalanced by cold contempt—that best shows the need for some further conversation about, but preferably with, Luther.

If so, the conversation can be worthwhile only if it is held under certain conditions. These conditions are suggested by

Gerhard Ebeling, one of the great Luther researchers of this century. In the preface to his book *Word and Faith*, Ebeling argues that anyone who enters such a conversation must listen to both the reformer and the contemporary world.

That is how conversation works. There must be listening—not the kind of half-eared attention which shares its space with preparations to answer, but that deep kind of hearing which lets the other be the other, even when the other is outspokenly outrageous and five centuries beyond his time. At the same time, there must be opportunity for reply—a chance to say "You're right" or "You're not only wrong, but dead wrong and dangerous."

Under these conditions a conversation with Luther can be fruitful for the irreligious and the religious alike. Whatever he may have in common with the twentieth-century world, Luther is a sixteenth-century man. That is part of his strength. He challenges what we take for granted, picking up aspects of daily life overlooked for their sheer commonness and placing them in a new light. It may also be part of his weakness. Much of what we assume is completely foreign to him. The conversation becomes productive in the mix—hearing the challenge he offers and arguing with it, letting the differences emerge and stand, listening and replying.

Finally, Luther is a man of faith. Whether lecturing to the monks, tacking up challenges to debate, leaning over the pulpit in the city church of Wittenberg, standing alone before the emperor, or rejoicing in the pigtails on his pillow, Luther understands himself first as a believer. To enter fairly into conversation with him is to let him be a believer, to let him bring his witness to Jesus Christ—not under obligation to accept or agree with what he says, but simply to listen.

The purpose of this little volume is to provide an entry into Luther's side of the conversation in the hope that such an exchange can be initiated, broadened, or continued. The first part of this book, therefore, is devoted to introducing Luther, providing enough information so that those entering the conversation for the first time, or reentering it, have at least a basic idea of who they are conversing with. The second part of the book lets Luther speak for himself in one of his own favorite writings, a writing that has established itself as a favorite among his literary legacy: the Small Catechism. An "afterword" provides some thoughts for continuing the discussion or conversation with Luther in today's world.

1
LUTHER'S LIFE

Until recently, Luther biographies generally have been as feisty and quarrelsome as Luther himself in some of his worst moments. Luther has been portrayed as either a son of the devil, fathered by an incubus, or as a prophet of deliverance, raised up at the end of days. Those who ventured between these two sides risked the wrath of both.

While "whys" and "wherefores" still provoke disagreements among Luther's biographers, interest in historical accuracy and ecumenical fairness have brought some calm to the situation. This calmness, however, should not be interpreted as a lack of interest in Luther, for in his middle years, between 1517 and 1530, Luther stood toe-to-toe with emperors and kings and contended with many of the forces that have shaped modern life. The great achievements of these middle years continue to arouse interest in both his youth and his later years.

THE YOUNG LUTHER
The land of Saxony, where Luther lived all his life, lies in what is now East Germany—southwest of Berlin, north and westerly along the Czech border. This area includes such great German cities as Leipzig, long a fur-trading and book-publishing center; Weimar, for a time the capital of the German republic; and Dresden, a manufacturing center. Luther spent his career as a preacher and teacher in a political division of the country called Electoral Saxony. The town where he grew up, Wittenberg, was the principal city in Electoral Saxony.

Saxony is much like western Pennsylvania or northern Minnesota—wooded and rolling, breaking in some places into open prairies suited for farming, but also rocky and craggy enough to provide resources for mining.

Unlike Pennsylvania or Minnesota or even the great shield region of Ontario, Canada, however, Saxony is a land of abandoned, though occasionally preserved, castles. In Luther's time and before, Saxony was one of the frontiers of Europe. Germany was divided into hundreds of small, often warring states and cities. Though knights were not the force they once had been, a few of them were still willing to defy the governmental leash. Castles commanded the military advantage of the hilltops, but some had already begun to decay. Cities and towns were usually walled, the citizens living in general readiness for warfare.

Luther's town, Wittenberg (or "White Mountain," in the language of some early settlers), is actually in flatland on the river Elbe. Story has it that someone, perhaps a misplaced prairie man or woman, took a white sand promontory to be something more than it actually was. At Luther's time, Wittenberg was a bustling center of 2,100 people—small by contemporary standards and still small compared to Leipzig or the even larger Cologne, but on a par with a number of other regional centers of the day. The countryside was full of smaller villages four or five miles apart.

Whatever else can be said for the city, Wittenberg did not have much of a reputation. The ruler of the other part of Saxony, one of Luther's fiercest enemies, dismissed both Luther and the town in a single sweep: "No church reform is going to come out of that hole."

According to contemporary accounts, there was some justice to Duke George's negative remark about the town. Wittenberg was small and narrow, spread out behind walls along the river. Most of its houses were small with thatched roofs; only a few people were able to afford slate roofs, which were the alternative to risking fire. The streets were narrow and only occasionally paved with stones. Besides giving passage, the streets provided a home for cows and pigs. Once in a while they were cleaned by the rains, but seldom by a shovel. Without lights, the streets were dingy, dirty, and dark.

The main buildings of Wittenberg were two large churches. The city church, where Luther frequently preached (one year he preached a total of 170 times), was on the town square, next to the courthouse. The other church was part of the castle of the political leader (the Elector) of Luther's part of Saxony. The castle church was down the street, about one long block from the town square. The original castle church was destroyed long ago. It has been rebuilt, and Luther's grave is in the front of it, below the pulpit.

Luther was not born in Wittenberg, and he did not die there. Both his birth and death took place in another town, Eisleben, to the west and somewhat north of Wittenberg.

Though Luther and his family were not always certain about the exact year, the best evidence is that he was born in 1483. His mother remembered the time of year—November 10—better than the year itself. Her name was Margarethe Lindemann. Recent research shows that she came from a fairly prosperous and well-educated family in the town of Eisenach. Her husband was Hans Luther, an independent miner who was ambitious to move up in the world.

Luther started school early—at the age of four and a half, by one recounting—and from the beginning prepared for further education. Grammar school was just that: studies in Latin, the language of the schools, the government, and the church. Latin was taught with the medieval equivalent of a dunce cap and a stick. The elderly Luther still remembered some of the lickings he received at the hands of his teachers.

Luther moved through a few different schools before going on to his mother's family town, Eisenach. There he studied rhetoric, music, and other subjects, in addition to his work in Latin. Legend tells of Luther singing in the streets and begging with other students, according to the tradition of the time. There is also the story of Frau Cotta, a friendly matron who cared for Luther at this time, perhaps as a friend of his family.

From Eisenach, Luther went farther east to the university at Erfurt. He was following in his father's plans, moving along toward studies in law. He finished his undergraduate degree and took a master's degree as well before starting law school in 1505. But then, so suddenly that his friends and family were taken by surprise, Luther became a monk.

There are a number of theories about Luther's sudden turn to the monastery. One is the famous story, told by Luther himself, of a vow spoken in the midst of a terrible thunderstorm: "Saint Anne help me, I will become a monk" (Saint Anne was the patron saint of miners). Other theories speak of the death of one of Luther's schoolmates the previous year, or of his own narrow escape with a knife wound suffered in a hunting accident. Whatever happened, Luther has the ultimate questions of his life and future raised for him, and he sought answers to them with the Augustinian hermits in the city of Erfurt. His father was not pleased.

Apparently Luther was an excellent monk, at least if his progress in the order is any indication. Hardly more than a year passed before he was ordained in one of the great cathedrals of Erfurt. He was taken under the gentle care of the German leader of his order, John von Staupitz, who selected him for further education and a teaching career. After various duties, including his studies and a trip by foot to Rome on monastic business, Luther received his doctor's degree in theology at Wittenberg in 1512.

The same year, he was appointed to the Wittenberg University faculty as a professor of biblical studies, a position he held for the rest of his life. The school was seven years old at the time and numbered only a few hundred students. Unlike modern universities, it had no real campus, but was spread out in a few buildings in the city.

In addition to his duties as a lecturer, Luther also preached in the monastery chapel and later the town church, supervised nine other monasteries, looked after the brewery licensed to the monks for the city, cared for the fishponds and other sources of meat for his men, and then, in addition to these and other duties, had to find time to study.

This hardly sounds like the life of a man languishing in self-doubts and uncertainty. Still, in spite of his study and hectic schedule, Luther continued to be troubled by the question that, probably more than anything else, had driven him to monkery.

This question, as Luther himself later defined it, was how to find a gracious God. Nowadays, when psychology is a favorite sport and even beginners count themselves as experts, it is easy to blow this question out of proportion. Luther asked what any person asks when brought up against this question: Who is it that holds my life and future? Is that person or power good or bad, kindly disposed or threatening? Or is there nothing holding me? Is the future completely empty?

If there was a difference in Luther, it was in the radical way in which he pursued the question. Early in his monastic life he turned upon himself, attempting to beat the question into submission with fasting and other disciplines. Additional monastic means of dealing with the question were equally unsatisfactory. The only real help came from his confessor, old Father Staupitz, who taught Luther to "look to the wounds of Christ" for consolation.

Staupitz's pastoral word, traditional as it may have been, changed the direction of Luther's quest. Luther had sought the solution to his question within himself—in his own disciplines, attitudes, and understandings. Staupitz, however, directed Luther away from himself. Then, in the course of his biblical studies in the Psalms and the letters of Paul (particularly Romans), Luther was moved still further. He had been taught to understand God passively. Now, in the Scriptures, he encountered the God who does not simply wait and watch but who, as the God of Abraham, Isaac, and Jacob, the one who raised Jesus from the dead, seeks, finds, saves, and delivers. This was the breakthrough. As Luther himself later recalled:

> At last, by the mercy of God, meditating day and night, I gave heed to the context of the words, namely, "In it the righteousness of God is revealed, as it is written, 'He who through faith is righteous shall live.' " There I began to understand that the righteousness of God is that by which the righteous lives by a gift of God, namely, by faith (*Luther's Works*, Vol. 34, p. 337).

These words, along with some other recollections of the older Luther, have sent scholars in search of a particular time between 1513 and 1520 and even a particular place (an old tower in the monastery at Wittenberg has been suggested) where this turnabout occurred. After extensive research and debate, however, it appears that the older Luther telescoped a gradual change into a sudden transformation. When one reads his lectures between 1513 and 1517 or 1518, a gradual development can be detected—not a sudden, once-for-all turnabout.

By 1518, however, it is clear that Luther was on to something at odds not only with monasticism but with some of the basic practices and confessions of the Catholicism of his time. He found himself in the midst of conflict.

THE REFORMER

The lure that drew Luther into controversy was a religious huckstering similar to what now happens on radio and television. The "evangelist" was an experienced Dominican salesman named John Tetzel. Instead of hankies, crosses that glow in the dark, or pictures of himself, Tetzel sold indulgences.

Technically, indulgences were more carefully defined. The medieval church claimed the right to impose specific penalties for sins. These penalties were to satisfy church requirements while also providing a form of discipline. Indulgences were given, also sold, to grant release from church penalties, and not to confer forgiveness. But paper definitions do not always hold in practice. Some of the more financially interested popes and other church officials found indulgences a fine money-raising scheme. And old hands like Tetzel did not bother with niceties—an indulgence purchase was declared the equal of forgiveness of sins, life, and salvation.

The issue for Luther was repentance. When Tetzel set up camp across the border near Wittenberg (Frederick the Wise, the Elector of Saxony, would not allow him to cross the border), people began returning to the city with indulgence letters, demanding that Wittenberg priests absolve them. To Luther, it was literally cheap grace—absolution sold at the going rate— rather than the free grace of Christ which brings repentance.

Luther published his *Ninety-Five Theses* on October 31, 1517, calling for discussion of the practice of indulgences in a public university debate. He sent a copy of his theses to the man responsible for the indulgence sale, the archbishop of Mainz. In the theses, Luther spelled out his basic conviction. "When our Lord Jesus Christ said, 'Repent,' " he wrote, "he willed our whole life to be one of repentance."

Luther soon found his hand in the corn picker. The archbishop forwarded the theses to Rome and the pope; friends and others sympathetic to Luther's arguments spread the theses all over Europe. Arm followed hand, and then shoulders, head, and the rest of Luther was caught up in a growing grind of controversy. For the next three and a half to four years, Luther would be the talk of Europe.

Luther wanted to discuss repentance, but church officials and those who supported them in the controversy had a different issue in mind. Their issue was the one dear to the hearts of bureaucrats of all times and all places, whether medieval or modern, and whether in Rome, Washington, or Moscow: *the proper channels of authority.* By calling into question the practice of indulgences, this monk-turned-Bible-professor had called into question the primacy, if not the infallibility, of the pope.

So Luther was put in the squeeze. His order, the Augustinian hermits, was asked to silence him. Luther replied by intensifying his theological challenge. With the controversy growing, one of the great Roman Catholic cardinals of the day—Thomas Cardinal Cajetan, outstanding theologian and papal diplomat—was dispatched to quiet Luther. Luther, however, rejected Cajetan's touch as paternal.

When the controversy threatened to get out of hand and damage the papacy, still another course was tried. This time Luther's prince, Elector Frederick the Wise, and through him Luther himself, was offered what amounted to a bribe. It was rejected.

So in 1520, Pope Leo X took his final recourse: Luther was ordered to submit within sixty days on pain of excommunication. When he failed to submit, he was excommunicated. Word of the excommunication finally reached him in January 1521.

Other reformers had arisen before Luther. Some of them, such as John Hus in Czechoslovakia a century earlier, became quite powerful in their calls. They had either been put to death, as Hus who was burned at the stake, or absorbed into the church machinery, as was the case with another contemporary of Luther, the great humanist Erasmus.

It looked as if Luther, under excommunication, might go the way of Hus. What saved him from this fate was political protection by his own prince and other reform-minded German leaders. Frederick the Wise was not always sure of Luther. He kept his distance. But he insisted that Luther could not simply be put away without being granted a fair hearing. And he was powerful enough in the German and European scheme of things to keep Luther in safety. As the controversy wore on and Luther gained even more support from German leaders, Frederick's protection became more sure.

Because of Frederick's protection, what had started as an invitation to debate a religious question and turned into a question of church authority now became a political question as well.

So with Frederick's diplomats working overtime, Luther was summoned to appear before the most important political assembly in Europe. Called a *diet,* this assembly included the heads of the German states and cities. Presiding over the diet was a man who bore the somewhat pretentious title of Holy Roman Emperor.

The emperor was from a powerful Austrian family, the house of Hapsburg. He was at the time king of Spain, but through family connections, he also had a power base in the Low Countries. With these holdings, he dreamed of a European dynasty for his family. He was not about to see Europe, which was already divided by so many political units, further split by a division in the church.

So while willing to hear Luther, Charles V, the emperor, was hardly sympathetic. He had papal legates at his elbow to make sure any sympathies that might arise would not get away.

The diet where Luther was finally to get his hearing was scheduled for the German city of Worms, thus to be remembered by its wonderful name: the Diet of Worms. The time was April 1521. Luther traveled by foot and cart under a pass which guaranteed him safe conduct on the condition that he not preach. In spite of this, Luther went west to Worms as a German hero, preaching all the way.

At Worms the great showdown finally took place. After much bobbing and weaving among the various factions, some trying to give Luther an open floor and others trying to keep him silent, Luther was finally brought before the emperor. He was asked if the controversial writings stacked before him were his own and if he would recant everything he had written. Acknowledging the writings to be his, Luther asked for a day to consider the diet's demand.

The next day, early in the evening, Luther was brought before the emperor and the assembled princes, city representatives, and papal officials. Though conditions had been imposed to render him silent, Luther's supporters had won this opportunity for him to address the leaders of his people. Luther spoke clearly and quietly, concluding in the famous words of his reform:

> Unless I am overcome by the testimony of Scripture or by clear reason (for I believe neither the pope nor councils by themselves), I remain conquered by the Scriptures which I have adduced. As long as my conscience is captive to the words of God, I neither can nor will recant, since it is neither safe nor right to act against conscience. God help me, Amen (Cited in Scott H. Hendrix, *Luther and the Papacy* [Philadelphia: Fortress Press, 1981], p. 133).

When Frederick the Wise saw the impasse at Worms, he began to worry about Luther's safety. Under his supporters' urging, Luther left Worms by night on horseback. As he and his escorts made their way back to Wittenberg, they were apprehended by other horsemen. Luther was seized and taken to an old castle high above his mother's family town of Eisenach. The castle was the Wartburg, and the horsemen had been employed by Frederick the Wise. After three and a half to four years of notoriety, Luther suddenly dropped from public sight.

Luther was used to a day brimming with activity; now he found himself with time on his hands. He grew a beard, did some hunting, and dressed as a knight, calling himself "Junker Georg." But he felt sorry for the deer and birds and thought of how the pope and the emperor were hunting for him. He became anxious and depressed, viewing his life as a battlefield of principalities and powers.

As the months wore on at the Wartburg, Luther finally settled on a project that would occupy him for the rest of his life. He had gotten hold of Erasmus's Greek New Testment, the first edition of a New Testament in medieval Europe that came anywhere close to the original text in the original language. For a number of centuries the Bible had been available only in Latin. Now, with access to the text of the New Testament in its original language, Luther set out to translate it into the language of his people, that is, into German.

When he began to translate, Luther worked at an incredible

pace, completing the entire New Testament in a matter of a few months. The translation was published in 1522 and is remembered as the "September Testament," after its publication date.

But Luther did not stop there. He was not yet satisfied with the New Testament translation, and the Old Testament, available through Jewish communities in the Hebrew text, awaited translation. Within six years, then, Luther managed to make the whole Bible available in translation. But still he continued to work on his translation, bringing together friends from the faculty of the University of Wittenberg to assist him.

Luther also found assistance for his translation in the butcher shops, stores, and on street corners. He went to the butchers, for example, to get the German names for animal parts mentioned in the sacrificial laws of the Book of Leviticus. Always he sought, as he said, to make the Bible speak like a German.

Luther had a superbly gifted sense of the language. His translation of the Bible became to the Germans what the King James Version became to English-speaking people. In fact, Luther's translation was even more in that it established him as the father of the modern German language.

The time at Wartburg had to end, if not for Luther's sake then for the sake of Wittenberg. While Luther was hidden away, more radical reformers were on the run in Wittenberg. Philipp Melanchthon, Luther's closest colleague, was not able to hold the line. Luther finally went back to his city in disguise in spring 1522.

Though there was some real risk in Luther's return to Wittenberg, a new political situation—a type of detente—had emerged following the Diet of Worms. This situation amounted to a five- or, if the Lutherans are counted, six-way tug of war with ropes going in all directions and Charles V trying to hold on to all of them in the middle.

The most powerful tug came from a great Turkish warrior named Suleiman the Magnificent. He roped in Budapest and nearly succeeded in getting Vienna during the 1520s and 1530s. Other combatants in this strange tug of war were the kings of France and, with a small yank rather than a big tug, of England; the popes; the Lutherans; and finally the Hapsburgs themselves. While trying to haul in one group, Charles always had to be contending with the others. The result was a standoff that held until shortly after Luther's death.

With Charles tied up in the middle and the other opponents fighting it out, Luther and the Lutherans—as they had come to be called—were left in peace. Only once in the remainder of his life did Luther get involved in the politics of the Reformation, and that was indirectly. This was at the Diet of Augsburg in 1530. But Melanchthon represented the Lutherans at this diet, and Luther stayed behind at Coburg about a day's journey away because the Elector did not want him risked in another encounter with the emperor.

This temporary freedom from the emperor, however, did not mean complete peace. There were theological battles to be fought, and there were other forces loose in Saxony.

Even before going to Worms, Luther had learned to use a magnificent new weapon: the printing press. It had been around awhile, but nobody had used it as Luther would. Sometimes the use was against his will—independent printers would pirate Luther's writings, occasionally right out of his office or lecture room, more often simply by reprinting what another printer had already offered. But Luther knew the medium, and he exploited it to the fullest. It is reported that at one point in the 1520s over one-half of the material in print in all of Europe was from Luther's pen.

Much of the material was polemical. In treatises published in small pamphlet form, Luther and his theological opponents exchanged blasts and counterblasts. It was a tough-talking age anyway, and the theologians were not bothered with considerations of gentility. Though Luther's crudeness is often exaggerated, he could compete with the best of them. The barnyard extended right to his doorstep so that resources for comparisons were always close at hand. This explains why Luther wrote treatises such as the one against the *Superchristian, Superspiritual . . . Goat Emser* or *Against Hans Wurst*.

Luther's writings were not just polemical. The printing press became another pulpit and lecture podium. So Luther published all kinds of shorter writings for church people, as well as commentaries and academic disputations. Some of his best-known works of these kinds are *The Freedom of a Christian*, the Small and Large Catechisms, and Luther's commentaries on the Magnificat and on the Book of Galatians.

The official collection of Luther's works, in the original Latin and German, is the Weimar Edition. It amounts to 119 large volumes, roughly equivalent to three or four sets of encyclopedias. A fifty-five-volume English translation of selected Luther writings is also available.

In 1525 another force broke loose in Germany—this time in and around Luther's backyard. For years, landholding German nobility and the peasant farmers and workers had lived in a precarious balance. A change in legal systems upset the balance, leaving the peasants with deep-rooted complaints.

Luther was sympathetic to the peasant cause and wrote against the abuses. But when some of the militants sought to justify their action in the name of the Reformation, insisting that revolt was required by the gospel, Luther objected. When open warfare broke out, he wrote an especially tough—not to say harsh—treatise urging the nobility to "stab, slay, and smite" the peasants who had risen up in arms. Whether justified or not, Luther's "harsh book against the peasants" —as he himself called it—cost the Lutheran reform heavily.

On top of all this—with Charles V only temporarily at bay, the peasants threatening, and trouble breaking out all around —Luther took another radical step: he got married. This was "to make the angels laugh and the devils weep," he said.

Other monks and many priests had begun to marry early in

the 1520s. In fact, Luther had helped arrange some of the marriages. His old monastery in Wittenberg, the Black Cloister, was nearly empty. Luther and another monk had been living there virtually alone.

In June of 1525, however, Luther made other arrangements. He had been helping to place through marriage a group of eight nuns who had escaped from a convent in the other part of Saxony by hiding in a drayman's herring barrels. There was one nun left who proved particularly difficult to place. After turning down one possible match, she announced that she would settle for one of Luther's old friends or for Luther himself. This nun's name was Katherine von Bora. She and Luther were married June 13. The remaining monk in the Black Cloister moved down the road and Frederick the Wise gave Luther and Katie the old monastery as their home.

Katie soon took over the household. She was a strong and gifted woman. Whereas Luther had a monk's sense of business and was compulsively generous and carefree about the results, Katie was a shrewd businesswoman. Luther filled up the house, throwing it open to students, homeless families, visitors from all over, and sick people from the community. Katie managed it, not only handling the family finances but finding new sources of income. She took over the monastery's old brewing license, for instance, and later bought a farm from her brother and ran it as well.

The marriage of Martin and Katie did not begin in any romantic way, but a deep love eventually grew out of it. Martin and Katie had six children, two of whom died as youngsters.

Evenings in the old cloister were often musical. In addition to everything else, Luther was an accomplished musician. He had a fine tenor voice, with such a range that some even describe him as an alto. He also played the lute, a difficult twelve-stringed medieval instrument the size of a guitar, and was knowledgeable enough to write harmony and to compose a number of hymns. Neighbors and students often came by in the evenings to play and to sing.

It must have been quite a household. Where cloistered monks had once walked in silent pairs, children now ran and shouted, students argued and kept a running written tab of Luther's irreverences, visitors came and went seemingly by the dozens, and everything was hustle and bustle.

Later on, students published their accounts of Luther's "table talk." These accounts are not always reliable, but they are full of humor and offer a sample of the daily life of the cloister, along with the insights.

THE OLDER LUTHER

Many Luther biographies, especially more recent ones, leave off around 1530. The last sixteen years of Luther's life were not as tension-filled or dramatic as the fiery years of the late teens and twenties. But there is much about these years that is of great interest.

One more attempt was made in Luther's later lifetime to close the division that had opened in the Reformation. Under heavy pressure from the emperor, a pope agreed to call a council of all the bishops of the church to see what might be done to effect reform. In preparation for such a council, Luther was asked to write a brief summary of the Lutheran witness. He replied with a document called the Smalcald Articles, an occasionally rambling but nevertheless clear and sharp confession of his faith.

While working on the Smalcald Articles late in 1536, Luther became very ill. Though he was able to travel to Smalcald, where the articles were to be discussed the next February, he was too sick actually to attend the meetings. In the inn where he stayed and on the way back to Wittenberg he almost died.

The problem at the time was kidney stones. He was completely blocked for several days, resulting in uremic poisoning which was so severe that the whites of his eyes became discolored. Though the blockage finally broke, perhaps as a result of a rough cart ride over rocky mountain roads, Luther had kidney difficulty the rest of his life. In fact, one recent biographer suggests that recurring bouts of uremic poisoning may explain Luther's irritability and some of the outrageous outbursts of his last years. In any case, Luther's health was broken. It had never been good, but now it turned even worse.

So Luther raged and roared, lashing out against the papists, the Jews, lawyers (a favorite target in his last years), and whoever else crossed his sights. Still, he had his wits about him. Some of his greatest work, such as the commentary on Genesis and the only recently carefully studied antinomian disputations, was written during this time.

Death finally came on February 18, 1546. With his sons and some students to escort him, Luther had gone to the town of Eisleben—his birthplace—to help settle a feud among some minor noblemen. After negotiating settlement, Luther went back to the inn where he was staying. He felt a sharp pain in his chest that evening which alarmed those who were with him. They stayed with him while he slept fitfully. At 2:00 A.M. Luther survived a second sharp pain in the heart, but when a third came sometime later, he died.

Luther's last written words were like comments in his lectures, a mixture of German and Latin: "Wir sind pettler: Hoc est verum"—"We are all beggars: this is the truth."

Luther's remains were returned to Wittenberg, where he was buried beneath the pulpit of the Castle Church. He was eulogized in funeral sermons as the prophet of Germany.

2

LUTHER'S WITNESS

One of the nicknames given to Luther and his early compatriots, besides the originally insulting taunt "Lutheran," was the "sola-ists." The latter word, which comes from the Latin word for "only," was intended partly as a barb. It was aimed at the Lutheran love for exclusive sayings, such as the word alone, grace alone, and faith alone.

Whatever else Luther might have been—monster of the medieval midway or prophet of the new age, heretic or reformer, co-father of acquisitive capitalism or herald of freedom—he most certainly was a preacher. He understood himself to have been called by God to be a witness of the gospel of Jesus Christ. Whether holed up in his office for the third straight sleepless night, off on a tirade in a lecture, climbing into the pulpit, visiting with friends, or playing with his family, this calling shaped Luther's life. So to get to know Luther to any degree at all, one must get to know his witness, that is, what, or better, who he stood for.

Does the old nickname provide a clue? Do the exclusive sayings provide an adequate basis for summarizing Luther's witness? Luther himself might want to argue otherwise had he the opportunity. He did not care for slogans any more than he liked the name Lutheran. Apparently he worried that when words become slogans, they lose their power. So Luther used and then dropped completely some phrases that were precious to him and have been considered characteristic of him, such as "theology of the cross" and "uses of the law." But these sayings—timeworn and dogeared as they may be—still have a way of breaking open the center of Luther's reflection on the hearing and telling of the freeing Word in Christ.

THE WORD ALONE

In short, enthusiasm clings to Adam and his descendants from the beginning to the end of the world. It is a poison implanted and inoculated in man by the old dragon, and it is the source, strength, and power of all heresy, including that of the papacy and Mohammedanism. Accordingly, we should and must constantly maintain that God will not deal with us except through his external Word and sacrament. Whatever is attributed to the Spirit apart from such Word and sacrament is of the devil (Smalcald Articles, p. 3, art. 8).

God's works are his words; he speaks and it is done: because the speaking and the doing of God are the same (Weimar Edition of Luther's Works, 3.152.7).

At the root of Luther's witness is a primitive, simple, and in-the-best-sense radical understanding of how words work. Words in general are power; the Word of God in particular is self-effecting, self-performing power.

The idea that words have a life of their own seems strangely out of place nowadays. This idea, however, may be found in the Bible, in stories such as Isaac's inability to withdraw his blessing from Jacob after the latter had tricked it out of him (Genesis 27), or Balaam's inability to curse the Isaelites (Numbers 23). It is also found among the villagers of today, who make up over 60 percent of the world's population and have not been as deeply effected by technology. Still, in the Western world today, which is awash in talk, most of it electronic, the notion that words are power sounds not only primitive but downright foolish.

There is a type of language, a part of everyday talk, that is particularly vulnerable. This is *significative* talk, the kind of communication where words are used as signs to signify or point to something or someone else. When a speaker uses words in this way, the hearer has to think about what the words say, identify, or require, and then respond or react accordingly.

Many different possibilities exist for a breakdown in such significative talk. When words are used as signs, there can be a breakdown in the speaker ("I know what I mean, but I can't say it"), between the speaker and the hearer ("Oh, is that what you meant?"), within the hearer ("How in the world am I supposed to do that?"), or against the speaker ("That's just not right!"). When attempts at manipulation and deception are mixed with the problems already caused by this kind of talk, it is no wonder that words get a poor reputation.

But there are also words, every bit as much a part of daily life, which are used precisely because of their power. They are *effective* words, words that make things happen. They are not as much significative as they are expressive. They set out hatred or anger or love or tenderness.

For example, words of love are just what they are called: "sweet nothings." Words like "sweetheart," "honeybun," or "sugarplum," if a person asks for a definition, are meaningless. But when they are spoken between lovers, they are full of power; they burst with warmth and joy, bestow a deep sense of sharing or belonging, and express love.

There can be breakdowns in effective words, too. They do not work automatically, as though they contained within themselves some sort of magic. But there is life and power in such words. They reach out and touch the hearer, making love, creating hope in despair, effecting trust in the place of fear, reshaping the future.

Luther did not begin with such general observations about how words work. Rather, he began with the hearing of one of them. And it was not just one of them, either—not as he came to understand it. It was *the* word of power, of freedom, and of a future in Christ.

The story of Luther's quest for a gracious God is often told with attention directed more to the quest itself than to what ended it. His quest has sometimes been viewed as a deep, psychological search full of anxieties and self-mortifications, scrupulous self-analysis, and unmet needs. Luther's own later rememberings feed this view, as he dramatized his dissatisfaction with traditional medieval remedies. But he tells such stories to speak of how his hunt ended and what continued to bring it to an end: the hearing of the effective Word of Scripture.

Luther had been taught to read the Scripture and to hear its message significatively. In fact, much of the scriptural word is significative, and Luther continued to hear and read it as such. The commandments and all that goes with them are the best example. They describe things to do and things to leave undone, setting out demands and prohibitions: "You shall have no other gods before me," "You shall not take God's name in vain," and so forth. The commandments are not the only words in the Bible that can work this way. Just about any one of the Bible's words can be a reminder of something to have or not have, to do or not do, to be or not be.

But there is an effective (not just a significative) Word in the Scripture as well, and Luther's turnabout came when it broke through in his hearing. This is the Word of gift and promise, of testament (in the sense of "last will and testament"), and of bestowal. In this Word, as Luther came to hear it, God goes beyond talk of expectations and rewards or punishments to express himself, to lay bare "his fatherly heart." It is in this sense that God's words are his work: he does what he says—expressing himself, freeing, releasing, and opening up the future by his talk.

An example of this can be found in one of Luther's favorite passages, John 16:33: "In the world you have tribulation; but be of good cheer, I have overcome the world." Even though this is not a commandment, it is possible to hear this word significatively: "Christians ought to be cheerful, even when the going gets rough." If the Scriptures were simply significative, that is what the message would be: another moralism grating across the ear like fingernails across a chalkboard.

But as Luther was brought to a hearing and a telling of this passage, he saw a promise in it, an effective Word in which Christ expresses himself, laying himself out to the hearer: "I have overcome the world." In the light of his victory, in view of the fact that he holds the future, cheer becomes not only possible but also a downright gift. It is like hearing your loved one profess love. You do not have to tell yourself to feel good about this; you simply do.

"The Word alone," as a saying of the reformers, is a declaration of the priority of this effective Word of witness for the church in its hearing and telling.

Luther was not worried about the word of God's expectations and requirements getting across. He would fight with anyone who tried simply to dismiss the law or write it off. But he was convinced that God's demands will make themselves known and felt in one way or another. If people do not hear the commandment against false gods, they will keep getting broken by false gods until they finally start wondering about the real one. If the preacher does not preach against stealing, the policeman will. If coveting becomes a way of life, the distrust that results will eventually cause enough trouble that people will start asking if it is really worth it. There is honor even among thieves. In short, there has never been an absence of moralists or of moralisms.

But the Word of God's self-giving in Christ—the Word that actually creates faith, engenders hope, and makes love—is something different. It is not in the workings of things as the law is. This Word is "alien" or "external," as Luther called it, a Word that comes from outside the hearer. Thus it cannot be possessed or taken for granted; it cannot be contained or assumed.

There are some indications, if not assurances, about where this Word is to be heard. Luther was convinced that this Word was to be heard in the Bible. The Bible is the original witness to Christ, the sure and certain source of the Word's declaration. So Luther virtually lived in the Scripture, working with it constantly.

In the same way, this effective Word of freedom in Christ could be heard from a neighbor. Here the written word of Scripture becomes a living Word, spoken by a real person. Whether on the lips of a preacher or at coffee with a friend, there is someone who can listen and reply, and so hear and tell.

The Word is also in the sacraments: baptism and the Lord's Supper. Armed with his understanding of the Word as God's self-expression, Luther attacked the medieval sacramental system of the church. He argued that God acts only in these sacraments through which he has promised to act.

Still, there is something elusive about the Word. It is in the Scripture, but some books of the Bible do not proclaim it as well as others. Luther argued that the Bible holds Christ, just as the manger held the baby Jesus. For that reason he could call the Book of James "the epistle of straw" and could criticize other books as well.

The elusiveness of the Word is evident also in one's neighbor. While the pastor or a friend in faith may be "the living voice of the gospel," it is also possible that they may not understand or know how to speak the gospel at a time when it is desperately needed.

Moreover, a person may become so preoccupied with participation in the sacraments that he or she experiences no sense of joy or release, but only routine and even boredom.

"The Word alone," one of the exclusive sayings of the Reformation, is keyed to both the power and the elusiveness of the effective Word of God's self-giving in Christ. It includes the conviction that God expresses himself to his creation in and through this Word alone, declaring himself to give all that he requires—to give even his very self. This Word alone creates faith, effects hope, and makes love, bringing these into being in such a way that the only possible parallels are God's creating out of nothing or God's raising Jesus from the dead.

Finally, in the end, only this Word is worth telling. And only this Word is worth the commitment, in the face of its elusiveness, to seek its telling.

GRACE ALONE

If you are asked, "What do you believe in the Second Article, concerning Jesus Christ?" answer briefly, "I believe that Jesus Christ, true Son of God, has become my Lord." What is it to "become a Lord"? It means that he has redeemed me from sin, from the devil, from death and from all evil. Before this I had no Lord and King but was captive under the power of the devil. I was condemned to death and entangled in sin and blindness. . . . Let this be the summary of this article, that the little word "Lord" simply means the same as Redeemer, that is, he who has brought us back from the devil to God, from death to life, from sin to righteousness, and now keeps us safe there (Large Catechism, Second Article of the Creed).

If there is such an effective, future-opening word in Scripture, the questions to be asked are already apparent: What is it? What does it say?

The classical Lutheran answer shows the grounds for Luther's own apprehension about catchwords and slogans, for the question is addressed in terms that provoke other questions. The effective, freeing Word is the Word that God saves by grace alone. But what is grace? A general policy of leniency? An attitude or disposition which inclines God to deal kindly with us? A willingness to accept people on the basis of unmerited favor?

Luther was restless with theories or ideas of grace—explanations of it where grace is treated as though it were simply a policy, a disposition, or a willingness. He sought to speak of it concretely, specifically, in the down-to-earth terms of the actual event or occurrence that grace is. So in the summary of the

Second Article from the Large Catechism, which was written around the same time as the Small Catechism but for a different purpose, he defines grace as a transfer of powers effected by Christ.

One of the crucial differences between Luther's understanding and the common assumptions of North Americans is in estimates of power. Luther was convinced that there are certain problems that just cannot be solved. The current assumption, though it has been modified by recent experience, is that every problem has a solution; if there is no solution, the problem is not worth talking about. Yet even with this assumption, there is a sense of powerlessness in the face of some difficulties, both personal and public.

Despair is an example. Not even Scandinavians, who have been accused (maybe with some justice) of having an affection for melancholy, want to get caught in despair. It is something to be avoided if possible, but sometimes it is not possible. Despair sets in, taking hold of a person in such a way that the person is totally gripped by it.

When despair comes, it shows a power of its own. In fact, the conviction that despair ought to be controllable, that "I shouldn't feel this way, and if only I could do such-and-such, I'd feel better," makes the despair worse. It becomes double despair, so that in addition to the original despair, a person begins to despair about despairing and then to despair about despairing about despairing. The experience becomes circular, an unbreakable, seemingly endless chase in which the despair feeds on itself.

The same sense of powerlessness is even more evident in public life. Despite all the official rhetoric about solving things "if only," there is the private sense that things are really getting out of hand—whether in state, province, nation, or world. Yesterday's solutions are today's problems; yesterday's reformers are today's paunchy, unyielding bureaucrats. But it is worse than that, for the inequalities work their way out in injustice and warfare, grinding out their victims in unspeakable suffering.

Luther describes this unyielding power, whether personal or public, in terms of an evil triumvirate of "sin, death, and the power of the devil." When Luther speaks of sin, he is not so concerned about what he called "puppy sins"—saying a bad word or having an extra glass of wine. Rather, he speaks of "unbelief, despair, and other great and shameful sins," as in the Small Catechism's explanation of the Sixth Petition of the Lord's Prayer. These are the sins of the first table of the Ten Commandments—the conviction that God does not have the future in hand either and that therefore other forms of protection, other sources of help and security, other gods, are to be preferred.

"Death and the devil" are in the same league. They are "powers and principalities," as Ephesians identifies them, which manifest themselves in their gripping, binding dominion. Death can be delayed, not prevented. The devil, far from being a pointy-tailed cartoon character, is that power which attacks the conscience, which hides itself in obsessions and compulsions that drive and control.

Describing the actual workings of grace, Luther speaks of a transfer of powers—of being taken from under the grip of evil forces and being placed under the dominion of Christ.

It is crucial for Luther that this transfer is not simply theoretical. While some later Lutherans turned it into such, Luther was not content with an "as if" or an "as though," a philosophical or theological exchange. He called one such attempt "a game played in an empty theater." Real powers require real opposition. Despair does not end theoretically by hearing explanations about it. It has to be stopped. In the same way, nobody can eat paper justice.

Then how does grace happen? Effecting the transfer, making

it actually and concretely possible, is the work of Christ. How specifically did he, or does he, do this? Here again Luther comes head up against the elusiveness of the freeing Word, and as usual he seeks to declare it in down-to-earth terms. So he uses different expressions, sifting through them in hopes of getting at the nub of it.

Luther's basic expression of the work of Christ is in terms of battle or warfare. Christ and the forces of evil meet each other in battle. Like a general who recognizes that he is the object of the conflict and that his troops will be safe from opposition only through his death, Christ laid down his life for his own.

Luther also speaks in terms that John von Staupitz used, describing the work of Christ as a royal wedding. In a marriage, husband and wife hold their property in common. So Christ gives his people what he has—his power over sin, death, and the devil. In turn, he receives what his people have—vulnerability to these forces. The result is the transfer.

In his 1535 *Commentary on Galatians,* Luther takes over an expression from the law courts. Because Jesus is a friend of sinners, when the sinners are picked up and accused of their crimes, Jesus is found in their company and arrested as an accessory after the fact. Thus he is exposed to the same opposition and condemnation as all the other sinners. But when the powers condemn him, they condemn themselves and all their condemnations. So, taking his friends along, Jesus is set free and at the same time frees them.

But all the expressions, images, or analogies finally break down, for the opposition—the evil triumvirate—functions in us, binding and tying us in such a way that we are the opposition. So Jesus must also take us on in such a way that he gets hold of our self-preoccupations, anxieties, obsessions, compulsions, and commitments. He has done this in his death. It is as though Jesus says, "I know that what you want is control, not only of me, but of all things. And I know you'll fight me as long as you haven't got such control, despairing and rebelling all along. So go ahead. Put me to death. See where it gets you.''

The resurrection then counts as God's own reply to the forces of evil within and outside us. By raising Jesus from the dead, God in effect says, ''See now, you can't get rid of me, for I am in charge here. You have no dominion over me. In Christ I am reclaiming all things for myself, including not only you but also the whole earth.''

For Luther, then, the transfer of powers for the individual is part of God's reasserting his power over all things. God is not simply concerned with individuals, as important as each person is. His grace is for the whole creation, to reclaim or restore everything. Justification and justice belong together, as gifts of God's grace.

At the same time, grace is always grace *alone* for Luther. This ''alone'' is both polemical and pastoral.

Polemically, the ''alone'' is set out against every attempt to try and combine God's work and human effort as working agents in the exchange of powers. Luther was trained in this kind of a theology, a system which said that if people do what they can, God will make up with grace for whatever they have not done. He understood it as the perennial temptation, to imagine that we are somehow in neutral territory and that we can or must help Jesus effect our own transfer. The ''alone'' here declares the complete sufficiency of Christ's work: he does not need help.

The ''alone'' is also declared for the sake of speaking a pastoral word of comfort. Anyone who has lived through an attack of anxiety knows how aggravating it can be to hear such words as ''Don't worry.'' Sign-words or words of law just make the anxiety worse. If it could be so simply commanded, worry would not be a problem. So the ''alone'' stands as a word of wisdom: when someone needs to hear a word of grace, do not tack conditions on it, but declare the effective Word *alone* of how God, through his grace alone, has taken on all powers and conditions and defeated them.

FAITH ALONE

Outwardly his grace seems to be nothing but wrath, so deeply is it buried under two thick hides or pelts. Our opponents and the world condemn it and avoid it like the plague or God's wrath, and our own feeling about it is not different *(Luther's Works,* vol. 14, p. 31).

Faith is a divine work in us that transforms us and begets us anew from God, kills the Old Adam, makes us entirely different people in heart, spirit, mind, and all our powers, and brings the Holy Spirit with it. Oh, faith is a living, busy, active, mighty thing, so that it is impossible for it not to be constantly doing what is good. Likewise, faith does not ask if good works are to be done, but before one can ask, faith has already done them and is constantly active. Whoever does not perform such good works is a faithless man, blindly tapping around in search of faith and good works without knowing what either faith or good works are, and in the meantime he chatters and jabbers a great deal about faith and good works. Faith is a vital, deliberate trust in God's grace, so certain that it would die a thousand times for it. And such confidence and knowledge of divine grace makes us joyous, mettlesome, and merry toward God and all creatures. This the Holy Spirit works by faith, and therefore without any coercion a man is willing and desirous to do good to everyone, to serve everyone, to suffer everything for the love of God and to his glory, who has been so gracious to him. It is therefore as impossible to separate works from faith as it is to separate heat and light from fire (Formula of Concord, Solid Declaration, art. 4).

If the Word is effective as a promise-bearing Word of grace, what shape does life take under its hearing? Luther answers in the seemingly almost contradictory terms of the two previous statements: it is a life marked by opposition and yet at the same time one that is joyously fruitful. It is a life lived "by faith alone."

Luther's own life, of course, was full of opposition. His struggles before the turnabout that came with his discovery of grace alone had their counterpart in the difficulties that beset him during the Reformation. Sometimes, in fact, he said that he could identify with Noah—wondering if he was completely alone in the world. Given the kind of animosity directed against him and some of the difficulties that beset the reform from within as well as from without, it is perhaps not so surprising that Luther should speak of opposition as a characteristic of life in faith.

Yet opposition is more than something simply personal. Luther found a theme running through the New Testament witness that generally is left dormant in good times, surfacing only when there is trouble. John 16:33, "In the world you have tribulation," is an example of this theme. Jesus' warning to his disciples that the servants' fate is not above their master's (Matt. 10:24–25) and Paul's references to being treated as the "off-scouring of all things" (1 Cor. 4:13) are other examples. The same theme is evident also in 1 Peter and Revelation.

Opposition has at least two different sources. One is the "sinful self," the old Adam, or, though the term is not as helpful, the old Eve. Though the transfer of powers has taken place in grace, the old rebellious self does not simply disappear into the past tense. It remains, worrying about the future, clamoring concerning its needs, demanding its dignity, and so forth. It is Pogo's old sense of having met the enemy, and it is us, only deepened and strengthened by the fact of Christ's unstinting self-giving.

With opposition from within, there is also opposition from without—from "the world." Among people who are convinced that the self can be achieved by grasping and acquiring and seeking control, a word that the true self comes only through self-loss is bound to appear not only contradictory but also downright foolish. Who can believe that a carpenter from the hill country of old Galilee who got himself executed for treason could be the one in whom the whole cosmos hangs together? In a world where children are maimed and murdered, as Ivan Karamazov once asked his brother Alyosha, who can believe anything at all?

In addition, there is the uncanny sense that the evil seems to be aimed, that there is some maliciously intelligent power which senses a person's point of greatest vulnerability and then unleashes its strength directly there.

So evil comes in triplicate. Whether it is "the devil, the world, and the sinful self" or "sin, death, and the power of the devil," faith always lives in jeopardy. Like a magnet, it draws its opposite.

Luther understood this continuing wrestling between faith and what opposes it in terms of the cross. Being brought under the power of a Lord who gains his dominion by being crucified, the believer shares in the same fate: death. So Luther speaks of faith as a daily dying with Christ. It is being brought to one's limits, discovering that there is no exit, realizing that there is no future in or of the self: the kind of thing that happens in and through suffering. It is being "conformed to the image of his Son," as Paul calls it in Rom. 8:29. Or, as Jesus himself spoke of it, it is taking up the cross and bearing it (Mark 8:34).

But with the cross, there is also resurrection. As strongly as Luther emphasized faith's opposition, he just as strongly celebrated faith's power, its incredible ability to stand in the face of what would overwhelm it and still bear its sweet fruits.

This was one of the real hot spots of the Reformation, and it has remained an issue since. Luther's critics argued, and still argue, that a person is justified when he or she believes the Word of grace in Christ *and* does good works accordingly. Luther argued that a person is justified or "becomes what Adam and Eve were meant to be," as he puts it, when he or she believes. This believing, the believing of faith which takes God at his word, will produce all the good works necessary.

The issue is one of agency. Who is the agent? Who takes

responsibility for the good works? To put it more sharply and to push the issue in Luther's favor, is it I or Christ in me (Gal. 2:20)?

Luther was convinced that faith is a life-determining power, somewhat on the order of a lover with the beloved. If a lover hears and believes the "I love you" of the beloved, nobody has to hang over the shoulder whispering, "Now you should be happy about this" or "You should think about how you might be helpful since this person feels so good about you." Lovers are happy, spontaneously joyful, giddy. And lovers cannot do enough for one another. Even after the giddiness has worn off, when the love has grown over years of togetherness, there is the quiet attentiveness—the gently familiar touch of a couple who have spent years together.

Or faith is on the order of a cancer patient who finally receives the all-clear. Recovering from such an illness, coming back from a similar brush with death, a person does not have to be told to savor life, to appreciate a spring breeze or the snap of a fall afternoon. If the person continued to act as though there were no tomorrow, griping and complaining, there would clearly be something overriding the release, stripping it of its fruit.

Faith's analogies are in the realm of such events as love and hope. But, finally, the only real analogy for faith is the resurrection of the dead. As Luther spoke of it, to be brought under the power of Jesus as Lord is to be given a new self, a new life. It is to be brought to the realization that the hands that hold the future are the same hands that touched the lame and the lepers and, in the end, took nails in them. It is to discover that the destiny of the self and of the whole earth is being shaped and is ultimately in the control of the one who raised Jesus from the dead and who has promised to give life to all who are with him.

This faith is freedom. It is "the end of the law," as Paul puts it in Rom. 10:4, for in Christ, the self does not have to be achieved or accomplished. There is a new self, a new agent.

Someone else has taken control. To live in faith is to live "in Christ," to be taken under the power of his efficacious Word so that all of life is shaped by his grace, in faith.

It is daily life that Luther speaks of here. In fact, Lennart Pinomaa, a great Finnish Luther scholar, has described the reformer as "the theologian of daily life" because of his down-to-earth way of seeing the gift that has been given in the midst of what is common and ordinary.

The tempter's seductive call is to dream of being something or somewhere else. It is to be convinced that being a believer is not enough, that there has to be something more. That something extra may be gotten only in some other place, where people are really concerned, where things are holier, where there are no dogs that whine, no children who howl, no phones that ring, no people who gripe, and so on.

But Luther insisted otherwise. Both the daily dying of the old self and the daily rising of the new self take place in the midst of what is daily and common.

The daily dying is as ordinary, but just as specific too, as an aching back, a frustrated hope, a child who cries in the night, a demanding neighbor, or an aging parent who needs care but cannot receive it graciously. Whatever draws us or propels us away from ourselves—toward the neighbor in love and toward Christ in faith—bears the mark of the cross.

By the same token, the resurrection of Jesus quickens and announces its presence in common services rendered—in backrubs, wiped noses, drinks of water, and down-to-earth virtues like patience, kindness, goodness, self-control—as well as in the most common of all things, the words of our mouths, suddenly armed to break forth, sighing, soaring, and then bursting in with the faith-making, freedom-bestowing Word of grace.

3

THE BACKGROUND OF LUTHER'S SMALL CATECHISM

The Small Catechism is one of those deceptively simple works that has a way of getting to the depths of things just because it is so simple. A person can learn it as a child, as generations of Lutherans have, and then come back to it as an adult to discover that it has a fresh and vital way of cutting through complexities to get to the nub of daily life.

How did this document come to be written? As usual, with sources born in the Reformation, the Small Catechism comes out of controversy. But the controversy related to this document was somewhat different. In this case the disputants were a pair of Luther's closest friends, and their disagreement was the first public quarrel within the Lutheran reform movement. The quarrel, however, had a good effect, for when Luther stepped in to settle the differences, he put his own hand to something he had long been talking about: the catechism.

TROUBLE IN WITTENBERG

In the middle of the 1520s, the Lutheran leaders finally obtained something they had been hoping for: the political authority to start reforming the congregations of the church in their own territories. They acquired this authority somewhat by accident. The emperor Charles V, had called a meeting and then could not make it because of a previous engagement with the Turks. In his absence, the Lutherans passed their own bill. But even if this authority may not have come quite legally, the Lutherans were determined to make the best of it.

Luther was ready with a suggestion of his own. He approached the prince of Saxony—who was at this time John, the brother of Frederick the Wise—suggesting that teams of parish visitors be set up to get firsthand information on the shape of the congregations. The teams would each be composed of two theologians and two lawyers, so that both the religious life and the social life of the parishes could be checked.

When the first visitation teams went out, they brought back some distressing reports. By contemporary standards, the conditions might not look so severe to us. But to the reformers, especially Philipp Melanchthon, the reports came as a shock. The most widespread problem was fornication by the preachers. Priests sworn to celibacy had found a way around this vow by taking on permanent, live-in "cooks." Up to 90 percent of the pastors in one district were living according to this arrangement. While the Lutherans no longer required celibacy of pastors, they did not support this particular solution to the problem.

Other problems encountered in the congregations were public and private drunkenness, disregard of the sacraments (one parish had not celebrated the Lord's Supper in eighteen months), and ignorance of the Word and outright contempt for it. In one parish, for example, the people had refused to memorize the Lord's Prayer because they considered it too long.

Even Luther, who was not generally oversurprised by evidence of sin, was moved to comment, "Good God, what wretchedness I beheld! The common people, especially those who live in the country, have no knowledge whatever of Christian teaching, and unfortunately many pastors are quite incompetent and unfitted for teaching" (from Luther's Preface to his Small Catechism).

Controversy grew out of the discussion of what to do about these conditions. Philipp Melanchthon was the language professor at the University of Wittenberg, teaching Greek and Hebrew, but he had also distinguished himself as a theologian.

Though the friendship between Melanchthon and Luther had been cool for a while, the two had reconciled their differences and had begun to work together closely.

By disposition and orientation, Melanchthon was something of a moralist. He once wrote to a friend the following remark that a leading contemporary scholar has taken as typical of him: "I never wanted to become engaged in theological work for any other reason than that I might contribute to the improvement of life" (quoted by Wilhelm Pauck in Vilmos Vajta, ed., *Luther and Melanchthon* [Philadelphia: Fortress Press, 1961], p. 17).

Looking at things this way, Melanchthon was horrified by the situation the parish visitors found. He proposed to deal with it as quickly and as efficiently as possible, by the means closest to hand: the law. So he wrote a draft of instructions for parish visitors, recommending that while also preaching the gospel, pastors had better proclaim the law in all its fullness—declaring the penalties to be expected not only in this life but also in the hereafter.

Luther and Melanchthon had another friend who, at this time (1528), was teaching in the town of Eisleben, where Luther was born. John Agricola had been a medical student who had come to Wittenberg early in the Reformation and had taken up with Luther and later with Melanchthon. He had been slated to join the faculty of the university in the 1520s, but remained in Eisleben until 1536, when he came to Wittenberg to teach theology.

Agricola sensed something afoul in Melanchthon's recommendations to the visitors. What happens to the gospel if there is such a quick retreat to the law? After rediscovering the liberating Word of Christ, should we then bring in the Ten Commandments and let them loose? Will not people then simply respond out of fear? And would not a repentance brought about by fear alone be false?

So Agricola recommended a different course. Rather than trying to solve the problem with the law, he argued that the gospel ought to be proclaimed "in all of its sweetness." As people hear it, they will be moved to repentance.

It was a summer of smoke. Though Luther himself did not get involved until near the end, the controversy became the talk of the Lutheran community. In fact, it became so well known that Melanchthon was contacted by Roman Catholic officials from Vienna who wondered if he would be interested in leaving Wittenberg and the Lutheran reform movement for a position in Austria.

Finally, in the fall of 1528, the Elector himself had had enough. He suggested that Luther take a hand in bringing his friends together again. Luther had thought the controversy was a war of words, and that it amounted to nothing more than the public's love of a fight. But when prodded by the Elector, he met with Melanchthon and Agricola and effected a compromise between them.

The net effect of the controversy was to convince Luther that he was going to have to put his own hand to writing a catechism. He had asked Melanchthon and Agricola each to write one. In fact, he had been suggesting this for years. But after the controversy and with some idea of what the results would be if he left the writing of a catechism to either, Luther decided that he would have to take on the assignment himself.

Luther was also convinced that Melanchthon and Agricola were both right and both wrong. The law has to be proclaimed—it could not simply be dismissed. But finally it was the gospel, the promise-bearing Word of Christ, that brings about repentance and new life.

THE CATECHISMS

Luther had two sources on which to draw when he went to work on the catechisms. One source was an old tradition of catechisms dating back to the early days of the church; the other was his own work earlier in the Reformation.

A number of catechisms had been written during the Middle Ages. Usually they contained the Apostles' Creed and the Lord's Prayer; often they included rituals for the praise of Mary and special prayers; sometimes they also had the commandments. In Luther's own vocabulary, "catechism" meant the Ten Commandments, the Apostles' Creed, and the Lord's Prayer in particular. The idea of taking these three together and providing explanations of the sacraments along with them was not necessarily new with Luther.

As he went to work to write the catechisms, Luther had some of his own work to draw on as well. Even before the Reformation had begun, he had already started preaching sermons on parts of the catechism. He continued this kind of preaching on a regular basis and, in addition, wrote a number of shorter works for people who were not professional theologians or pastors. He once wrote a little work for his barber, for instance, who had asked for help on how to pray.

Armed with these sources, Luther decided to do two catechisms—each intended for a different group of people.

Already in May, before the controversy of the summer had really started, Luther had begun to preach a series of sermons on the Ten Commandments. His series was interrupted, but he picked it up again in September. Going on to include other parts of the catechism, he continued again in winter, finally completing it in March 1529. The sermons became the basis of what was at first called the "German Catechism" and later became known as the Large Catechism. It was published in Wittenberg in April 1529 and was intended for pastors and teachers to use in their own study and preparation.

Never one to confine his attention to a single project, Luther dropped work on the Large Catechism to work on the Small Catechism in December 1528. He alternated back and forth between the two catechisms while also lecturing and carrying on any number of other duties. Still, he was able to complete the Small Catechism in May 1529. It was published first in pamphlet form and later on wall charts that could be hung in the home. Luther wrote the Small Catechism for parents to use in the instruction of their children.

The innovative feature of the catechisms is their sequence, beginning with the Ten Commandments, then moving through the Apostles' Creed to the Lord's Prayer and the sacraments. As Luther explained it, this sequence was to show the movement from the law to the gospel, from God's demand to the Word of promise and the new life that Word engenders. He said:

> There are three things which everyone must know to be saved. First, he must know what he ought to do and what he must leave undone. Then, as he has discovered what is impossible for him to accomplish by his own strength, he must know where to obtain, where to seek and find the power that will enable him to do his duty. And, in the third place, he must know how to seek and obtain that aid (Quoted by J. Michael Reu and John C. Mattes in *Luther's Small Catechism: A Jubilee Offering* [Minneapolis: Augsburg Publishing House, 1929], p. 15).

Although they share this common sequence, the two catechisms differ mainly in the fact that they were written for different groups of people. In the Large Catechism, which was written for pastors and teachers, Luther develops his explanations further and is sometimes sharper or more polemical than in the Small Catechism. At one point, for instance, he suggests that people who will not confess their sins, not yet realizing that the gospel is "mild and gentle," are "pigs . . . unworthy to appear in the presence of the Gospel or to have any part of it" (Large Catechism, Confession). But despite the occasional explosion, the Large Catechism is carefully measured and almost conversational in tone.

The Small Catechism is frequently noted for its gentleness. Luther was convinced that any reformation worthy of the name was dependent on the declaration of the Word to all who had ears to hear. So the language is direct, to the point without being blunt, simple without being patronizing, gentle without ever turning to mush. To paraphrase and apply to Luther what a

Russian doorman once said to John Steinbeck about the Russian language, the catechism has the earth in its mouth.

Luther was proud of his catechisms. Speaking of them together as though they were one and the same, he wrote to another reformer who wanted to publish Luther's collected works that he should forget it all, except his writing *The Bondage of the Will* and the catechisms (see *Luther's Works,* vol. 50, pp. 172–73).

Luther's own somewhat modest pride in the catechisms was certainly supported by how they were received. The two catechisms quickly became some of the most important writings of the reform. Portions of the Large Catechism were regularly read aloud during services in Lutheran territories; the practice of committing the Small Catechism to memory also soon become a feature of Lutheran parish life.

Over the centuries the Large Catechism, due perhaps more to its gifted younger colleague than to any fault of its own, has been increasingly forgotten. But when people find it, it still has a way of turning suddenly explosive. For all its age, the Large Catechism can be astonishingly contemporary, both for its theological insights and for some of the comments on perennial social problems.

But the Small Catechism, with its gentleness and simple sophistication, has really stolen the hearts of Lutherans. Other confessions may be placed alongside it, constitutions and matters of church order may occasionally supersede it, and there may be some rare complaints heard about it, but the Small Catechism keeps popping up to close its gentle grip once again. Johann Sebastian Bach wrote a cantata for it; some of the greatest thinkers in Germany and the Scandinavian countries memorized it as children; it came to North America in old trunks and eager immigrant heads; it is cursed by confirmation kids and remembered with love by elderly people as they face their last moments. Five centuries later, it is still the way to remember Luther's birthday—to remember him so that he can be forgotten, hidden behind the freedom-bestowing Word.

4

THE SMALL CATECHISM

Explaining Luther's Small Catechism is somewhat like explaining a joke: both hearer and teller come to regret it, and the fun is taken away. But when the story is 450 years old, if not even older, there might be a need for at least some filling in. Perhaps, however, this can be provided in a way that allows the story still to have its fun about it.

THE COMMANDMENTS

Reasons for the sequence of topics in the Small Catechism may have been apparent to Luther, but nowadays it raises all kinds of questions. In fact, it may be the most controversial feature of the catechism. If the liberating Word of the gospel is what set Luther and the Reformation going, why does the catechism begin with the commandments? Is not this a kind of manipulation, making people feel bad with the commandments so that they can be made to feel better again by the gospel Word of the Apostles' Creed? Do not the Ten Commandments have something good to say as well? Does not putting them first inevitably put the gospel into a legal framework?

The questions spill out all over, but they come down to one: Why begin here? Luther's answer, instead of being predictable, turns out to be one of the most surprising features of the catechism—even though it is hidden in the background.

In other writings, Luther boldly dismissed any notion that the Ten Commandments are obligatory for Christians. The freedom of the gospel is freedom from the law—the law of the commandments as well as any other. So even after writing the catechisms, Luther could say that the whole task of Christian theology is to learn to ignore the law, works, and all active righteousness (See *Luther's Works*, vol. 26, p. 6).

In the same way, Luther objected to attempts to impose the commandments on Christians simply because they are in the Bible. The commandments certainly are biblical, he acknowledged (see Exodus 19 and 20), but a basic rule of thumb in Bible reading is to see who is being addressed. The commandments were given to the people of Israel, not to the church. So they are for the Jews, not necessarily for Christians. Arguing this way, Luther compared the commandments to the local laws of Saxony. One community's laws do not necessarily hold in another community, where customs and conditions may be different.

With these two quick strokes, then, Luther wiped out the most common assumptions about the commandments' coming first in the catechism. A basic question, however, remains: Why are the commandments in the catechism at all?

Luther's answer to this question was based on the conviction that there is what might be called a web of human interrelatedness, a basic way in which things work, which unites all people. One feature of this web is that people are made in such a way that no matter who, what, when, or where they are, there has to be someone or something they can count on. Nobody is self-contained. Every person has to have something—whether it is completely outside themselves or an ability within themselves that works on other people—to count on for help, support, and safekeeping.

The example that Luther used in explaining the First Commandment in the Large Catechism was money. People who rely on their money look to money to help them get whatever they need or to care for them in times of trouble. Money thus becomes their god, an idol.

Luther's conviction was that life works this way: whether it is

the God of Abraham, Isaac, and Jacob, or some little god,
everyone has to have one—even if that god is their own talents
and abilities.

By the same token, Luther argued, life is arranged in such a
way that people have neighbors. Whether living in a hermitage
or in a downtown area, whether faithful or unbelieving,
whether rich or poor some contact with other people is necessary. And in these contacts, there are certain indispensable
features: a person must be able to get along with others and, to
do that, must observe certain elementary rules.

As common-sensical as these observations may be, Luther
continued, they are obscured by sin. In times of trouble, people
admit they need help; until then, they try to do it alone. "You
shalls" and "you shall nots" always seem to apply best to other
people; only when we are caught red-handed do they also apply
to us.

Working from these convictions, Luther put the commandments into the catechism. He did this to show the web of
human interrelatedness, how things actually work among people, and how things are meant to work. The commandments
break through the obscurity of sin, clarifying what sin seeks to
cover. Since people must have a god, they should have the true
God, use his name for what it is intended, and take time to rest
and hear his Word. And since people have to have neighbors,
they should know what it takes to get along: decent homes to
get a good start in life, protection from killing, true friendships,
faithful marriages, respect for property, good names, and
trustworthy communities.

The commandments are in the catechism, then, not because
they are "Christian" or biblical, but because they show how life
works for everyone—the basic, elementary conditions needed so
that life may be lived.

This also explains why the commandments come first. The
catechism begins with the commandments because life begins
with the commandments. They are first in the order of ex-

perience. Before hearing the Word of promise, before baptism, before anything else, there is a world arranged and ordered by "you shalls" and "you shall nots."

Following are the commandments and their explanations as they appear in the Small Catechism.

THE TEN COMMANDMENTS

*in the plain form in which the head of the family
shall teach them to his household*

THE FIRST

"You shall have no other gods."
What does this mean?
Answer: We should fear, love, and trust in God above all things.

THE SECOND

"You shall not take the name of the Lord your God in vain."
What does this mean?
Answer: We should fear and love God, and so we should not use his name to curse, swear, practice magic, lie, or deceive, but in every time of need call upon him, pray to him, praise him, and give him thanks.

THE THIRD

"Remember the Sabbath day, to keep it holy."
What does this mean?
Answer: We should fear and love God, and so we should not despise his Word and the preaching of the same, but deem it holy and gladly hear and learn it.

THE FOURTH

"Honor your father and your mother."
What does this mean?
Answer: We should fear and love God, and so we should not despise our parents and superiors, nor provoke them to anger, but honor, serve, obey, love, and esteem them.

The Fifth

"You shall not kill."

What does this mean?

Answer: We should fear and love God, and so we should not endanger our neighbor's life, nor cause him any harm, but help and befriend him in every necessity of life.

The Sixth

"You shall not commit adultery."

What does this mean?

Answer: We should fear and love God, and so we should lead a chaste and pure life in word and deed, each one loving and honoring his wife or her husband.

The Seventh

"You shall not steal."

What does this mean?

Answer: We should fear and love God, and so we should not rob our neighbor of his money or property, nor bring them into our possession by dishonest trade or by dealing in shoddy wares, but help him to improve and protect his income and property.

The Eighth

"You shall not bear false witness against your neighbor."

What does this mean?

Answer: We should fear and love God, and so we should not tell lies about our neighbor, nor betray, slander or defame him, but should apologize for him, speak well of him, and interpret charitably all that he does.

The Ninth

"You shall not covet your neighbor's house."

What does this mean?

Answer: We should fear and love God, and so we should not seek by craftiness to gain possession of our neighbor's inheritance or home, nor to obtain them under pretext of legal right, but be of service and help to him so that he may keep what is his.

The Tenth

"You shall not covet your neighbor's wife, or his manservant, or his maidservant, or his ox, or his ass, or anything that is your neighbor's."

What does this mean?

Answer: We should fear and love God, and so we should not abduct, estrange, or entice away our neighbor's wife, servants, or cattle, but encourage them to remain and discharge their duty to him.

Conclusion

What does God declare concerning all these commandments?

Answer: He says, "I the Lord your God am a jealous God, visiting the iniquity of the fathers upon the children to the third and the fourth generation of those who hate me, but showing steadfast love to thousands of those who love me and keep my commandments."

What does this mean?

Answer: God threatens to punish all who transgress these commandments. We should therefore fear his wrath and not disobey these commandments. On the other hand, he promises grace and every blessing to all who keep them. We should therefore love him, trust in him, and cheerfully do what he has commanded.

THE CREED

Heard in their personal address, the commandments have a way of doing exactly what Luther said. First, they can make a person angry. This is true not only of the commandments but also of Luther's treatment of them.

Many things about both can be maddening. The First Commandment and Luther standing behind it are confident they know the difference between false gods and the true God. But how do they know for sure? The commandments and Luther behind them are clearly rural and patriarchal; theirs is a world of two-parent families living out their years in a nuclear way, a world where virtually everyone marries, where the neighbor spoken of is clearly a "he" and "the wife" comes right between the house, the servant, and the cattle.

At the same time, there is something deeply appealing here.

If a person is going to have to have a god of some kind, it should be the right one. It follows that this god should be called upon for help and direction, and that this god ought to be listened to in the affairs of every day. As long as people live in communities, it follows that homes ought to be stable, life respected, marriages faithful, property and good names protected. With allowances for the kinds of changes in conditions Luther himself acknowledged as necessary, it follows that even if we no longer regard wives as property and do not commonly own cattle, coveting still destroys the trust necessary for getting along with our neighbors.

The commandments also do what Luther was convinced they do: they accuse, driving people to despair. Reading such a simple, commonsense, and just detailing of daily life drives a person to ask: Why does it not work that way? And, in addition, why do I not work that way? Just because the commandments are so down-to-earth, firm-handedly fair, and good, they turn a pointed finger at us.

Here, then, Luther moves to the Apostles' Creed—the confession of faith that was most commonly used in the church at that time as now. The explanations of the three articles of the creed—concerning Father, Son, and Holy Spirit—are hardly more than a few sentences in length. But they bristle and boom, verbs piling on top of verbs, and adverbs tumbling over the nouns and adjectives in a seemingly breathless attempt to say everything at once. The explanation of the Second Article of the creed, which is one long sentence, has been called the most beautiful sentence ever written in the German language.

For all their activity and beauty, however, the explanations are also remarkably subtle. The whole weight comes to rest in a gentle interplay of the small words such as *ought, may,* and *has.*

In his explanation of the First Article of the creed, Luther begins with what has been implicit in his treatment of the commandments: the gifts of daily life. He understands this giftedness as built into the web of things, as part and parcel of how things work—whether for believers or unbelievers. People are "gifted," doing easily and without apparent strain what others cannot do even with their best efforts. People are "born under the right star" or "have it handed to them" or are "lucky" or "fortunate." Even in what we pay for, there is gift: for example, the sunshine, rain, good soil, and a farm family's sacrifice in the wheat that has become flour in a loaf of bread.

This giftedness, in Luther's explanation, supplies the basis for an *ought:* therefore we ought to "thank, praise, serve, and obey him."

Once more, the ought is in the nature of things. Because of getting something for nothing and receiving far more than has been paid for, it is only reasonable to indicate some appreciation. And if the gifts keep right on coming, as they do, then it only makes sense to be of service—not only to the Giver, but also to others who may not have received as much.

As reasonable as this might be in theory, it is often something different in practice. Here the *ought* becomes the focal point of rebellion, for if God has given us what we need, there are always things we do not have; if he has guarded and protected us in time of danger, there are still threats and troubles that may turn out to be overwhelming; if sharing with our neighbors is a good idea, the good Lord should find out just what kind of neighbors live next door, and then he would know something different.

Luther considered the First Article of the creed the most difficult to believe. Why? Because it states that everything happening to us takes place under God's supervision. That means we are placed square under the ought, agreeing that it is only right, yet fighting against it.

In the Second Article, the ought is transformed into something entirely different: a *may*. This happens through the transfer of powers in which Jesus Christ becomes "our Lord."

As mentioned in the earlier chapter on Luther's witness, his concern here is to speak of a change that actually takes place. Redemption, a word with its roots in the process of releasing someone from salvery, is as real as rebellion against obligations to God and our neighbor. Redemption happens as a person is taken hold of, grasped, and held by the power of the One who really does love his enemies—who meets every attempt at self-justification by taking it up into himself and repaying evil with good. As the Word of this One, Jesus of Nazareth, the destined Lord of all, comes home to a person, it exposes all our self-preoccupations and breaks them, raising up a new person who takes Jesus at his word. This is an end and a new beginning, a death and a resurrection.

So the *ought* becomes a *may*. What has been an external demand, impinging on and provoking self-concern, fear, and rebellion, now becomes another gift—an even better one. Incorporated into the self-giving of Christ, becoming one of his beneficiaries, a person may "live under him in his kingdom, and serve him in everlasting righteousness, innocence, and blessedness." A new situation has been created, new possibility has actually been given.

But now this statement is followed with one of the most surprising and, in the true sense of the word, radical statements in the catechism: the explanation of the Third Article of the creed. This article declares that though there is nothing we have done or can do to make the new life happen, it *has* actually become a reality in us. *Has* is the pivotal word.

What the Third Article describes has been compared to mopping-up action toward the end of a war. The decisive victories have been won and the spoils taken, but the enemy has not yet laid down its arms. There are battles remaining to be fought.

So while the transfer has taken place and the *may* has been established, the new life remains in jeopardy. The old self rises up in anxiety and fear, demanding immediate release, desperate for itself. Faith wrestles with unbelief, and unbelief is capable of gaining the upper hand. So there is push and pull.

Yet amid the hiddenness of daily life, it *has* happened. Luther was convinced that the new life in Christ, brought about by the Spirit, always has this hiddenness about it. The new life will remain hidden until the last day, but what is hidden is nevertheless still real. In spite of everything, people actually come to faith and give themselves in daily service.

The church, too, participates in this hiddenness. Luther described the words of the Third Article, "I believe in . . . the holy catholic Church, the communion of saints," as an article of faith like any other. We believe what is said and confessed here even though we cannot see it. We believe in the church, the fellowship of the godly, which has no outwardly distinguishing mark about it other than this. Yet within this fellowship, the freedom-bestowing, future-opening Word is spoken, and gifts that make service in the wider community possible are given.

In this sense Luther says that the creed teaches where to obtain, to seek, and to find the power that will enable us to do our duty. Through the work of the triune God, who meets us in both gift and ought, the rebellion is brought to its end and a new person is raised up "to be what Adam and Eve were meant to be, only better."

Following are the articles of the Apostles' Creed and their explanations as they appear in the Small Catechism.

THE CREED

*in the plain form in which the head of the family
shall teach it to his household*

THE FIRST ARTICLE: CREATION

"*I believe in God, the Father almighty, maker of heaven and earth.*"

What does this mean?

Answer: I believe that God has created me and all that exists; that he has given me and still sustains my body and soul, all my limbs and senses, my reason and all the faculties of my mind, together with food and clothing, house and home, family and property; that he provides me daily and abundantly with all the necessities of life, protects me from all danger, and preserves me from all evil. All this he does out of his pure, fatherly, and divine goodness and mercy, without any merit or worthiness on my part. For all of this I am bound to thank, praise, serve, and obey him. This is most certainly true.

THE SECOND ARTICLE: REDEMPTION

"And in Jesus Christ, his only son, our Lord: who was conceived by the Holy Spirit, born of the virgin Mary, suffered under Pontius Pilate, was crucified, dead, and buried: he descended into hell, the third day he rose from the dead, he ascended into heaven, and is seated on the right hand of God, the Father almighty, whence he shall come to judge the living and the dead."

What does this mean?

Answer: I believe that Jesus Christ, true God, begotten of the Father from eternity, and also true man, born of the virgin Mary, is my Lord, who has redeemed me, a lost and condemned creature, delivered me and freed me from all sins, from death, and from the power of the devil, not with silver and gold but with his holy and precious blood and with his innocent sufferings and death, in order that I may be his, live under him in his kingdom, and serve him in everlasting righteousness, innocence, and blessedness, even as he is risen from the dead and lives and reigns to all eternity. This is most certainly true.

THE THIRD ARTICLE: SANCTIFICATION

"I believe in the Holy Spirit, the holy Christian church, the communion of saints, the forgiveness of sins, the resurrection of the body, and the life everlasting. Amen."

What does this mean?

Answer: I believe that by my own reason or strength I cannot believe in Jesus Christ, my Lord, or come to him. But the Holy Spirit has called me through the Gospel, enlightened me with his gifts, and sanctified and preserved me in true faith, just as he calls, gathers, enlightens, and sanctifies the whole Christian church on earth and preserves it in union with Jesus Christ in the one true faith. In this Christian church he daily and abundantly forgives all my sins, and the sins of all believers, and on the last day he will raise me and all the dead and will grant eternal life to me and to all who believe in Christ. This is most certainly true.

THE LORD'S PRAYER

When Luther originally wrote the Small Catechism, he planned to include a special section on what he had spoken of earlier in the Reformation as a "theology of the cross." When he went to work on the catechism, however, he found the theology of the cross so clearly expressed in the Lord's Prayer that he dropped his original plan.

In recent years, the phrase "theology of the cross" has become something of a slogan. When it becomes a catch phrase, it is treated as an insider's wisdom or kind of theology of champions. And then it is just the opposite of what Luther was talking about, for the theology of the cross, as he spoke of it, is a theology that reflects on the suffering of daily life in order to speak the liberating Word within it. It speaks of the hiddenness of God, of the way God sustains his people in the midst of brokenness, and of suffering with and for the neighbor in the unavoidable difficulties of daily life. Suffering is not to be sought; neither is it to be hidden from.

The conviction that God gives his gifts in the hiddenness of everyday things shapes Luther's explanations to the Lord's Prayer. So in explanations to each petition of this prayer, there is a sense of opposition, a sense of a power or force that must be overcome.

God's name is hallowed or kept holy when those who would distort his promise-bearing Word are restrained; his kingdom comes as he overcomes us in the power of his Spirit; his will is done when he hinders and defeats the triumvirate of sin, death, and the devil; daily bread is given in spite of the hardness of heart that takes it for granted; forgiveness is declared against all the forces that would obscure it; help in temptation is provided in opposition to powers such as unbelief and despair; and deliverance from evil occurs finally only at the last hour—until then, we and ours remain exposed to it.

So the Lord's Prayer, as Luther explains it, is the prayer of the tempted. It is a prayer for those who live in the midst of a mopping-up action, where faith stands in continuing jeopardy. The Lord's Prayer expresses the hope of faith that these powers will be constrained, overcome, and finally routed.

At the same time that he emphasizes the continuing force of opposition, however, Luther also underscores the way that God enables the believer to stand in the face of it. Woven through the explanation of each petition is the assertion that God in fact does what is being asked without being asked: his "name is holy in itself," the "kingdom of God comes of itself," his will is done "without our prayer," he "provides daily bread, even to the wicked." Where this assertion is not explicit in the Small Catechism, as in the petition concerning forgiveness, it is emphasized in the Large Catechism. It is this conviction, that God does all these things without being asked, that makes possible the request that he also do them "among us."

In this way, the explanations to the Lord's Prayer stress the all-encompassing self-giving of God in daily life. Because he stands against it, the opposition that exists can be acknowledged. Because he will finally overcome it, we learn how to seek and obtain that aid necessary to pray in the face of it.

Following are the petitions of the Lord's Prayer and their explanations in the Small Catechism.

THE LORD'S PRAYER

*in the plain form in which the head of the family
shall teach it to his household*

"*Our Father who art in heaven.*"
What does this mean?
Answer: Here God would encourage us to believe that he is truly

our Father and we are truly his children in order that we may approach him boldly and confidently in prayer, even as beloved children approach their dear father.

THE FIRST PETITION

"Hallowed be thy name."

What does this mean?

Answer: To be sure, God's name is holy in itself, but we pray in this petition that it may also be holy for us.

How is this done?

Answer: When the Word of God is taught clearly and purely and we, as children of God, lead holy lives in accordance with it. Help us to do this, dear Father in heaven! But whoever teaches and lives otherwise than as the Word of God teaches, profanes the name of God among us. From this preserve us, heavenly Father!

THE SECOND PETITION

"Thy kingdom come."

What does this mean?

Answer: To be sure, the kingdom of God comes of itself, without our prayer, but we pray in this petition that it may also come to us.

How is this done?

Answer: When the heavenly Father gives us his Holy Spirit so that by his grace we may believe his holy Word and live a godly life, both here in time and hereafter forever.

THE THIRD PETITION

"Thy will be done, on earth as it is in heaven."

What does this mean?

Answer: To be sure, the good and gracious will of God is done without our prayer, but we pray in this petition that it may also be done by us.

How is this done?

Answer: When God curbs and destroys every evil counsel and purpose of the devil, of the world, and of our flesh which would hinder us from hallowing his name and prevent the coming of his kingdom, and when he strengthens us and keeps us steadfast in his Word and in faith even to the end. This is his good and gracious will.

THE FOURTH PETITION

"Give us this day our daily bread.

What does this mean?

Answer: To be sure, God provides daily bread, even to the wicked, without our prayer, but we pray in this petition that God may make us aware of his gifts and enable us to receive our daily bread with thanksgiving.

What is meant by daily bread?

Answer: Everything required to satisfy our bodily needs, such as food and clothing, house and home, fields and flocks, money and property; a pious spouse and good children, trustworthy servants, godly and faithful rulers, good government; seasonable weather, peace and health, order and honor; true friends, faithful neighbors, and the like.

THE FIFTH PETITION

"And forgive us our debts, as we also have forgiven our debtors."

What does this mean?

Answer: We pray in this petition that our heavenly Father may not look upon our sins, and on their account deny our prayers, for we neither merit nor deserve those things for which we pray. Although we sin daily and deserve nothing but punishment, we nevertheless pray that God may grant us all things by his grace. And assuredly we on our part will heartily forgive and cheerfully do good to those who may sin against us.

THE SIXTH PETITION

"And lead us not into temptation."

What does this mean?

Answer: God tempts no one to sin, but we pray in this petition that God may so guard and preserve us that the devil, the world, and our flesh may not deceive us or mislead us into unbelief, despair, and other great and shameful sins, but that, although we may be so tempted, we may finally prevail and gain the victory.

THE SEVENTH PETITION

"But deliver us from evil."

What does this mean?

Answer: We pray in this petition, as in a summary, that our Father in heaven may deliver us from all manner of evil, whether it affect body or soul, property or reputation, and that at last, when the hour of death comes, he may grant us a blessed end and graciously take us from this world of sorrow to himself in heaven.

[CONCLUSION]

"*Amen.*"

What does this mean?

Answer: It means that I should be assured that such petitions are acceptable to our heavenly Father and are heard by him, for he himself commanded us to pray like this and promised to hear us. "Amen, amen" means "Yes, yes, it shall be so."

THE WORD AND THE SACRAMENTS

If the Lutheran Reformation is a movement of the Word alone, why is there not a section in the catechism on the Word? Why does the catechism immediately jump to the sacraments?

While there is no separate section on the nature of the Word, there are three parts of the catechism devoted to declaring it: the Ten Commandments, the Apostles' Creed, and the Lord's Prayer. There is a word that demands, and through its demands it also constrains and accuses; there is the promise-bearing, life-granting Word of the gospel. The first three parts of the catechism declare both.

But we are not yet finished with the Word, as the explanations of baptism and the Lord's Supper make clear, it is not the elements—the water or the bread and wine—which make the sacraments work. Rather it is God's Word with the water, God's Word put together with the eating and the drinking. The sacraments are events of the Word—God's Word taking on the particulars of such common and earthly things to express itself "for you."

This concrete "for-you-ness" of the sacraments is their most crucial feature as far as Luther is concerned. The Word, too, is powerful and personal. Yet in the sacrament God takes hold of the water, the bread, and the wine to make the Word as particular, down-to-earth, and unambiguously inescapable as possible. "I baptize you, by name, in the name of the Father, Son, and Holy Spirit." "This cup is the new testament in my blood, poured out *for you* and for many for the remission of sin."

The *for you* is so decisively important because of the situation in which faith lives: in jeopardy. It is always possible to wonder if the promise-bearing Word is a word for you, if God actually does have you in particular in mind. The sacraments are his answer. He rubs unbelief's nose in the earthy stuff of the sacraments and says, "Here it is—for you!"

This is how faith and the sacraments go together. The sacraments require faith. If a person does not believe that God is at work in baptism and the Lord's Supper, that person obviously is not going to treat them as anything more than rites or customs. But the sacraments also give what they require, effecting the faith they demand. So a person may receive the Lord's Supper, full of wonder and questions about it, and still come away strengthened and helped. It is in the down-to-earth hearing and receiving of the "for you" that faith is born, nourished, and sustained.

Baptism is the sacrament of birth and new birth. By this means, God declares the baptized to be his own. And in this declaration he bestows all the gifts of the gospel. He gets out ahead of himself to express what the fate of the child or adult being baptized will be, even in the Last Judgment: forgiveness of sins, deliverance from death and the devil, eternal salvation. It is the beginning of a life marked by the movement of the Spirit, bringing about repentance and faith.

Following is the section on baptism from the Small Catechism.

THE SACRAMENT OF HOLY BAPTISM

*in the plain form in which the head of the family
shall teach it to his household*

FIRST

What is Baptism?

Answer: Baptism is not merely water, but it is water used according to God's command and connected with God's Word.

What is this Word of God?

Answer: As recorded in Matthew 28:19, our Lord Christ said, "Go therefore and make disciples of all nations, baptizing them in the name of the Father and of the Son and of the Holy Spirit."

SECOND

What gifts or benefits does Baptism bestow?

Answer: It effects forgiveness of sins, delivers from death and the devil, and grants eternal salvation to all who believe, as the Word and promise of God declare.

What is this Word and promise of God?

Answer: As recorded in Mark 16:16, our Lord Christ said, "He who believes and is baptized will be saved; but he who does not believe will be condemned."

THIRD

How can water produce such great effects?

Answer: It is not the water that produces these effects, but the Word of God connected with the water, and our faith which relies on the Word of God connected with the water. For without the Word of God the water is merely water and no Baptism. But when connected with the Word of God it is a Baptism, that is, a gracious water of life and a washing of regeneration in the Holy Spirit, as St. Paul wrote in Titus (3:5-8), "He saved us by the washing of regeneration and renewal in the Holy Spirit, which he poured out upon us richly through Jesus Christ our Saviour, so that we might be justified by his grace and become heirs in hope of eternal life. The saying is sure."

FOURTH

What does such baptizing with water signify?

Answer: It signifies that the old Adam in us, together with all sins and evil lusts, should be drowned by daily sorrow and repentance and be put to death, and that the new man should come forth daily and rise up, cleansed and righteous, to live forever in God's presence.

Where is this written?

Answer: In Romans 6:4, St. Paul wrote, "We were buried therefore with him by baptism into death, so that as Christ was raised from the dead by the glory of the Father, we too might walk in newness of life."

CONFESSION AND ABSOLUTION

Here, right between baptism and the Lord's Supper, is one of the catechism's big surprises: a section on private confession. Confession is not practiced today by Lutherans as it once was, up to the eighteenth century. Still, not only the catechism but also the Augsburg Confession (the catechism's counterpart as principal confessions of Lutheranism) both insist on it.

The concern in confession and absolution is the same as in the sacraments: that God's Word be declared to people in as concrete and as personal a way as possible. So it remains, though not commonly used, another way in which faith is supported and nourished in the midst of daily life.

Following is the section on confession and absolution from the Small Catechism.

[CONFESSION AND ABSOLUTION]

How Plain People Are to Be Taught to Confess

What is confession?

Answer: Confession consists of two parts. One is that we confess our sins. The other is that we receive absolution or forgiveness from the confessor as from God himself, by no means doubting but firmly believing that our sins are thereby forgiven before God in heaven.

What sins should we confess?

Answer: Before God we should acknowledge that we are guilty of all manner of sins, even those of which we are not aware, as we do in the Lord's Prayer. Before the confessor, however, we should confess only those sins of which we have knowledge and which trouble us.

What are such sins?

Answer: Reflect on your condition in light of the Ten Commandments: whether you are a father or mother, a son or daughter, a master or servant; whether you have been disobedient, unfaithful, lazy, ill-tempered, or quarrelsome; whether you have harmed anyone by word or deed; and whether you have stolen, neglected, or wasted anything, or done other evil.

Please give me a brief form of confession.

Answer: You should say to the confessor: "Dear Pastor, please hear my confession and declare that my sins are forgiven for God's sake."

"Proceed"

"I, a poor sinner, confess before God that I am guilty of all sins. In particular I confess in your presence that, as a manservant or maidservant, etc., I am unfaithful to my master, for here and there I have not done what I was told. I have made my master angry, caused him to curse, neglected to do my duty, and caused him to suffer loss. I have also been immodest in word and deed. I have quarreled with my equals. I have grumbled and sworn at my mistress, etc. For all this I am sorry and pray for grace. I mean to do better."

A master or mistress may say: "In particular I confess in your presence that I have not been faithful in training my children, servants, and wife to the glory of God. I have cursed. I have set a bad example by my immodest language and actions. I have injured my neighbor by speaking evil of him, overcharging him, giving him inferior goods and short measure." Masters and mistresses should add whatever else they have done contrary to God's commandments and to their action in life, etc.

If, however, anyone does not feel that his conscience is burdened by such or by greater sins, he should not worry, nor should he search for and invent other sins, for this would turn confession into torture; he should simply mention one or two sins of which he is aware. For example, "In particular I confess that I once cursed. On one occasion I also spoke indecently. And I neglected this or that," etc. Let this suffice.

If you have knowledge of no sin at all (which is quite unlikely), you should mention none in particular, but receive forgiveness upon the general confession which you make to God in the presence of the confessor.

Then the confessor shall say: "God be merciful to you and strengthen your faith. Amen."

Again he shall say: "Do you believe that this forgiveness is the forgiveness of God?"

Answer: "Yes I do."

Then he shall say, "Be it done to you as you have believed. According to the command of our Lord Jesus Christ, I forgive you your sins in the name of the Father and of the Son and of the Holy Spirit. Amen. Go in peace."

A confessor will know additional passages of the Scriptures with which to comfort and to strengthen the faith of those whose consciences are heavily burdened or who are distressed and sorely tried. This is intended simply as an ordinary form of confession for plain people.

THE LORD'S SUPPER

One of the most important words for understanding the Lord's Supper does not appear in our translation of the Small Catechism. Neither is it found any longer in Lutheran liturgies of the sacrament. This is the word *testament,* a word used to translate the Greek word which is sometimes rendered "covenant"—as, for example, "This cup is the new testament [or covenant] in my blood."

Luther emphasized the word testament as he did the name "Lord's Supper," because this word clarifies the direction of the sacrament, that is, who gives and who receives. In a *will,* the more current name for a *testament,* the deceased bestows his or her belongings upon the beneficiaries. There is no payment involved, even if the tax collector attempts to collect later. The testator gives, and the heirs receive.

The name "Lord's Supper" illustrates the same basic character of the sacrament. Though the catechism speaks of it by another name, the Sacrament of the Altar, and more recent usage has shifted toward the term "Eucharist," in fact the historic name among Lutherans is this one. The name "the Lord's Supper" shows whose supper it is, who the host is, who takes responsibility for the meal, and who carries it out.

This is crucial to Luther's explanation because the Lord's Supper is the sacrament of the tempted. Those who have been in faith's struggles with fear and anxiety know how deadly it can be to be told to help yourself. The crucified and risen Lord does things differently; instead of throwing us back on ourselves, he gives himself, declaring all that is his to be ours. "Here I am, now you have me—this is my body, given for you. I will never let you go, everything that I am is for you—this cup is the new testament in my blood, given for you and for many for the remission of sin.''

Following is the section on the Lord's Supper from the Small Catechism.

THE SACRAMENT OF THE ALTAR

in the plain form in which the head of the family shall teach it to his household

What is the Sacrament of the Altar?

Answer: Instituted by Christ himself, it is the true body and blood of our Lord Jesus Christ, under the bread and wine, given to us Christians to eat and to drink.

Where is this written?

Answer: The holy evangelists Matthew, Mark, and Luke, and also St. Paul, write thus: ''Our Lord Jesus Christ, on the night when he was betrayed, took bread, and when he had given thanks, he broke it, and gave it to the disciples and said, 'Take, eat; this is my body which is given for you. Do this in remembrance of me.' In the same way also he took the cup, after supper, and when he had given thanks he gave it to them, saying, 'Drink of it, all of you. This cup is the new covenant [testament] in my blood, which is poured out for many for the forgiveness of sins. Do this, as often as you drink it, in remembrance of me.' ''

What is the benefit of such eating and drinking?

Answer: We are told in the words ''for you'' and ''for the forgiveness of sins.'' By these words the forgiveness of sins, life, and salvation are given to us in the sacrament, for where there is forgiveness of sins, there are also life and salvation.

How can bodily eating and drinking produce such great effects?

Answer: The eating and drinking do not in themselves produce them, but the words ''for you'' and ''for the forgiveness of sins.'' These words, when accompanied by the bodily eating and drinking, are the chief thing in the sacrament, and he who believes these words has what they say and declare: the forgiveness of sins.

Who, then, receives this sacrament worthily?

Answer: Fasting and bodily preparation are a good external discipline, but he is truly worthy and well prepared who believes these words: "for you" and "for the forgiveness of sins." On the other hand, he who does not believe these words, or doubts them, is unworthy and unprepared, for the words "for you" require truly believing hearts.

EVERYDAY WORSHIP

For Luther, as for Paul before him, worship and work always went hand in hand. In fact, the word *liturgy* includes both notions, as does the English word *service*. To be taken under the dominion of Christ is not to be turned into some super-spiritual person who, in Luther's famous characterization of one of his opponents, "stares at the creation like a cow looking at a new gate." Rather, to be under the dominion of Christ is finally and for the first time to be brought down to earth. It is to be released for the daily round God had in mind for Adam and Eve in the first place—a round shaped by faith, by love of the neighbor, and by care for the earth.

So Luther's catechism does not end where many contemporary editions of it do, that is, after the explanation of the Lord's Supper. Rather, it goes on to suggest daily prayers, grace at the table, and the duties of the day. Faith makes us at home in the common things of life—in the routine of getting up, eating meals, living in families, doing the work of the day, going to bed.

There are, then, three more parts of the Small Catechism, each devoted to one of these aspects of the day. These parts now follow.

[MORNING AND EVENING PRAYERS]

How the head of the family shall teach his household
to say morning and evening prayers

In the morning, when you rise, make the sign of the cross and say, "In the name of God, the Father, the Son, and the Holy Spirit. Amen."

Then, kneeling or standing, say the Apostles' Creed and the Lord's Prayer. Then you may say this prayer:

"I give Thee thanks, heavenly Father, through thy dear Son, Jesus Christ, that Thou hast protected me through the night from all harm and danger. I beseech Thee to keep me this day, too, from all sin and evil, that in all my thoughts, words, and deeds I may please Thee. Into thy hands I commend my body and soul and all that is mine. Let thy holy angel have charge of me, that the wicked one may have no power over me. Amen."

After singing a hymn (possibly a hymn on the Ten Commandments) or whatever your devotion may suggest, you should go to your work joyfully.

In the evening, when you retire, make the sign of the cross and say, "In the name of God, the Father, the Son, and the Holy Spirit. Amen."

Then, kneeling or standing, say the Apostles' Creed and the Lord's Prayer. Than you may say this prayer:

"I give Thee thanks, heavenly Father, through thy dear Son Jesus Christ, that Thou hast this day graciously protected me. I beseech Thee to forgive all my sin and the wrong which I have done. Graciously protect me during the coming night. Into thy hands I commend my body and soul and all that is mine. Let thy holy angels have charge of me, that the wicked one may have no power over me. Amen."

Then quickly lie down and sleep in peace.

[GRACE AT TABLE]

*How the head of the family shall teach his household
to offer blessing and thanksgiving at table*

[BLESSING BEFORE EATING]

When children and the whole household gather at the table, they should reverently fold their hands and say:

"The eyes of all look to Thee, O Lord, and Thou givest them their food in due season. Thou openest thy hand; Thou satisfiest the desire of every living thing."

(It is to be observed that "satisfying the desire of every living thing" means that all creatures receive enough to eat to make them joyful and of good cheer. Greed and anxiety about food prevent such satisfaction.)

Then the Lord's Prayer should be said, and afterwards this prayer:

"Lord God, heavenly Father, bless us, and these thy gifts which of thy bountiful goodness Thou hast bestowed on us, through Jesus Christ our Lord. Amen."

[THANKSGIVING AFTER EATING]

After eating, likewise, they should fold their hands reverently and say:

"O give thanks to the Lord, for he is good; for his steadfast love endures forever. He gives to the beasts their food, and to the young ravens which cry. His delight is not in the strength of the horse, nor his pleasure in the legs of a man; but the Lord takes pleasure in those who fear him, in those who hope in his steadfast love."

Then the Lord's Prayer should be said, and afterwards this prayer:

"We give Thee thanks, Lord God, our Father, for all thy benefits, through Jesus Christ our Lord, who lives and reigns forever. Amen."

TABLE OF DUTIES

*consisting of certain passages of Scriptures, selected
for various estates and conditions of men, by
which they may be admonished to do
their respective duties*

BISHOPS, PASTORS, AND PREACHERS

"A bishop must be above reproach, married only once, temperate, sensible, dignified, hospitable, an apt teacher, no drunkard, not violent but gentle, not quarrelsome, and no lover of money. He must manage his own household well, keeping his children submissive and respectful in every way. He must not be a recent convert," etc. (1 Tim. 3:2–6)

DUTIES CHRISTIANS OWE THEIR TEACHERS AND PASTORS

"Remain in the same house, eating and drinking what they provide, for the laborer deserves his wages" (Luke 10:7). "The Lord commanded that those who proclaim the gospel should get their living by the gospel (1 Cor. 9:14). "Let him who is taught the word share all good things with him who teaches. Do not be deceived; God is not mocked" (Gal. 6:6, 7). "Let the elders who rule well be considered worthy of double honor, especially those who labor in preaching and teaching; for the scripture says, 'You shall not muzzle an ox when it is

treading out the grain,' and 'The laborer deserves his wages' "
(1 Tim. 5:17, 18). "We beseech you, brethren, to respect those who
labor among you and are over you in the Lord and admonish you, and
to esteem them very highly in love because of their work. Be at peace
among yourselves" (1 Thess. 5:12, 13). "Obey your leaders and submit to them; for they are keeping watch over your souls, as men who
will have to give account. Let them do this joyfully, and not sadly, for
that would be of no advantage to you" (Heb. 13:17).

GOVERNING AUTHORITIES

"Let every person be subject to the governing authorities. For there
is no authority except from God, and those that exist have been instituted by God. Therefore he who resists the authorities resists what
God has appointed, and those who resist will incur judgment. He who
is in authority does not bear the sword in vain; he is the servant of God
to execute his wrath on the wrongdoer" (Rom. 13:1-4).

DUTIES SUBJECTS OWE TO GOVERNING AUTHORITIES

"Render therefore to Caesar the things that are Caesar's, and to
God the things that are God's" (Matt. 22:21). "Let every person be
subject to the governing authorities. Therefore one must be subject,
not only to avoid God's wrath but also for the sake of conscience. For
the same reason you also pay taxes, for the authorities are ministers of
God, attending to this very thing. Pay all of them their dues, taxes to
whom taxes are due, revenue to whom revenue is due, respect to
whom respect is due, honor to whom honor is due" (Rom. 13:1, 5-7).
"I urge that supplications, prayers, intercessions, and thanksgivings
be made for all men, for kings and all who are in high positions, that
we may lead a quiet and peaceable life, godly and respectful in every
way" (1 Tim. 2:1, 2). "Remind them to be submissive to rulers and
authorities, to be obedient, to be ready for any honest work" (Tit.
3:1). "Be subject for the Lord's sake to every human institution,
whether it be to the emperor as supreme, or to governors as sent by
him to punish those who do wrong and to praise those who do right"
(1 Pet. 2:13, 14).

HUSBANDS

"You husbands, live considerately with your wives, bestowing
honor on the woman as the weaker sex, since you are joint heirs of the
grace of life, in order that your prayers may not be hindered" (1 Pet.

3:7) "Husbands, love your wives, and do not be harsh with them" (Col. 3:19).

WIVES

"You wives, be submissive to your husbands, as Sarah obeyed Abraham, calling him lord. And you are now her children if you do right and let nothing terrify you" (1 Pet. 3:1, 6).

PARENTS

"Fathers, do not provoke your children to anger, lest they become discouraged, but bring them up in the discipline and instruction of the Lord" (Eph. 6:4; Col. 3:21).

CHILDREN

"Children, obey your parents in the Lord, for this is right. 'Honor your father and mother' (this is the first commandment with a promise) 'that it may be well with you and that you may live long on the earth' " (Eph. 6:1–3).

LABORERS AND SERVANTS, MALE AND FEMALE

"Be obedient to those who are your earthly masters, with fear and trembling, with singleness of heart, as to Christ; not in the way of eye-service, as men-pleasers, but as servants of Christ, doing the will of God from the heart, rendering service with a good will as to the Lord and not to men, knowing that whatever good anyone does, he will receive the same again from the Lord, whether he is a slave or free" (Eph. 6:5–8).

MASTERS AND MISTRESSES

"Masters, do the same to them, and forbear threatening, knowing that he who is both their Master and yours is in heaven, and that there is no partiality with him" (Eph. 6:9).

YOUNG PERSONS IN GENERAL

"You that are younger, be subject to the elders. Clothe yourselves, all of you, with humility toward one another, for 'God opposes the proud, but gives grace to the humble.' Humble yourselves therefore under the mighty hand of God, that in due time he may exalt you" (1 Pet. 5:5, 6).

WIDOWS

"She who is a real widow, and is left all alone, has set her hope on God and continues in supplications and prayers night and day; whereas she who is self-indulgent is dead even while she lives" (1 Tim. 5:5, 6).

CHRISTIANS IN GENERAL

"The commandments are summed up in this sentence, 'You shall love your neighbor as yourself' " (Rom. 13:9). "I urge that supplications, prayers, intercessions, and thanksgivings be made for all men" (1 Tim. 2:1).

Let each his lesson learn with care
And all the household well will fare.

AFTERWORD

If there is to be some sort of continuing conversation with Luther, as suggested in the "Foreword," what shape might it take? Gerhard Ebeling has suggested that the conversation should be one where Luther can challenge the contemporary world while at the same time allowing the contemporary world (including us) to challenge Luther. This way there is give and take, listening as well as talking, and therefore the possibility of a real exchange.

But before such a conversation can proceed, some consideration should be given to questions that may be involved. What follows, then, is one example of a question that deserves to be considered in our ongoing conversation with Luther—the question of freedom.

To begin with, it should be noted that the American melting pot has a way of turning its corrosive juices loose on religions as well as on nationalities. So the historic faiths of Christendom—Roman Catholicism, Calvinism, and Lutheranism—have had great trouble maintaining themselves with much integrity here.

A number of the problems that have been raised concerning Luther actually reveal more about this melting pot than they do about Luther. Broadly stated, these problems are maintained on the basis of secondary authorities, and they reach their real point when it is argued that Luther should be dismissed on these "secondary" bases. Thus Luther is condemned as a "proto-Nazi" or is accused of having no social consciousness or is treated as one of the founders of capitalism.

Even a quick reading of some of Luther's writings and his history, however, is usually enough to show that these kinds of questions do not have much basis in fact. They are a kind of academic propaganda, slogans thrown out to dismiss rather than to encourage careful thinking.

Nevertheless, at the same time, there are important questions raised about Luther that reflect and require some things worth pursuing. Such questions, even when they challenge the Lutheran witness right to its core, should be especially welcome.

One such question concerns freedom. "The freedom of the gospel" was basic for Luther. His treatise *On the Freedom of the Christian* was crucial to the Reformation and remains one of his classical writings. In fact, early in his work, he occasionally followed the Renaissance custom of taking a Greek or Latin name that sounded much like Luther but meant freedom.

Freedom is an important word nowadays, too. In countries like the United States, Canada, and Australia, freedom is spoken of as part of the essential character of these nations. More than that, freedom is taken as something that makes us human.

But there is a critical difference between Luther's understanding of the word and contemporary discussions of it. Luther understood freedom as freedom *from* the self; much of contemporary discussion understands freedom as freedom *for* the self. Luther understood freedom as being for Christ, the neighbor, and the earth; in contemporary talk, freedom is often spoken of as freedom to choose a god, to get along on one's own, and to avoid entanglements.

Where do these two different understandings of freedom come together? What makes them so different? How do they work out in terms of the community? These are big questions. Yet they have a way of gripping both Luther and the culture in which we live right at dead center, right at their presuppositions. With such questions, the conversation with Luther can once again be productive.